FATIMA'S THIRD SECRET
Explained

Thomas W. Petrisko

FATIMA'S
THIRD SECRET
Explained

THOMAS W. PETRISKO

St. Andrew's Productions

CONSECRATION AND DEDICATION

This book is consecrated to Our Lady of the Rosary, who came to Fatima with a plan for peace. It is dedicated to Michael Fontecchio, one of Our Lady's chosen warriors for her coming Triumph.

Copyright © 2001 by Dr. Thomas W. Petrisko
All Rights Reserved

ISBN: 1-891903-26-8

Published by:

St. Andrew's Productions
6111 Steubenville Pike
McKees Rocks, PA 15136

Phone: (412) 787-9735
Fax: (412) 787-5204
Internet: www.SaintAndrew.com

Scriptural quotations are taken from The Holy Bible —RSV: Catholic Edition. Alternate translations from the Latin Vulgate Bible (Douay Rheims Version —DV) are indicated when used. Some of the Scriptural quotations from the New American Bible: St. Joseph Edition, The New American Bible— Fireside Family Edition 1984-1985, The Holy Bible—Douay Rheims Edition, The New American Bible— Red Letter Edition 1986.

PRINTED IN THE UNITED STATES OF AMERICA

ACKNOWLEDGMENTS

I wish to thank those most helpful to me during the writing of this book: Dr. Frank Novasack, Michael Fontecchio, Carole McElwain, Carol Jean Speck, Thelma Bugansky, Chris Pelicano, John Haffert, and the prayer group at the Pittsburgh Center for Peace.

Again, I thank my family for their support and understanding, my wife Emily, daughters Maria, Sarah, Natasha, Dominique, son Joshua, and our newest family member, Jesse, born October 13th, 2001. As always, a special thank you to my mother and father, Andrew and Mary Petrisko and my uncle, Sam.

ABOUT THE AUTHOR

Dr. Thomas W. Petrisko was the president of the *Pittsburgh Center for Peace* from 1990 to 1998 and he served as the editor of the Center's nine special edition *Queen of Peace* newspapers. These papers, primarily featuring the apparitions and revelations of the Virgin Mary, were published in many millions throughout the world.

Dr. Petrisko is the author of seventeen books, including: **The Fatima Prophecies**, *At the Doorstep of the World;* **The Face of the Father**, *An Exclusive interview with Barbara Centilli Concerning Her Revelations and Visions of God the Father;* **Glory to the Father**, *A Look at the Mystical Life of Georgette Faniel;* **For the Soul of the Family;** *The Story of the Apparitions of the Virgin Mary to Estela Ruiz,* **The Sorrow, the Sacrifice and the Triumph;** *The Visions, Apparitions and Prophecies of Christina Gallagher,* **Call of the Ages, The Prophecy of Daniel, In God's Hands,** *The Miraculous Story of Little Audrey Santo,* **Mother of The Secret, False Prophets of Today, St. Joseph and the Triumph of the Saints, The Last Crusade, The Kingdom of Our Father, Inside Heaven and Hell** and **Inside Purgatory** and **Fatima's Third Secret Explained.**

The decree of the **Congregation for the Propagation of the Faith** (AAS 58, 1186 - approved by Pope Paul VI on 14 October 1966) requires that the *Nihil Obstat* and *Imprimatur* are no longer required for publications that deal with private revelations, apparitions, prophecies, miracles, etc., provided that nothing is said in contradiction of faith and morals.

The author hereby affirms his unconditional submission to whatever final judgment is delivered by the Church regarding some of the events currently under investigation in this book.

TABLE OF CONTENTS

FOREWORD 1
INTRODUCTION 3

1 - WHY DOES MARY APPEAR? 13
2 - THE PHENOMENON OF MARIAN SECRETS 19
3 - NINETEENTH CENTURY VISIONS OF MARY .. 25
4 - THE FATIMA PROPHECIES 35
5 - THE CONTROVERSIAL 'THIRD PART'
    OF THE SECRET 41

THE MESSAGE OF FATIMA
   Theological Commentary by Cardinal Joseph Ratzinger 49

6 - ST. MICHAEL AND THE FLAMING
    SWORD OF FATIMA 79

EPILOGUE - 'MEN MUST CEASE OFFENDING GOD' .. 83

APPENDIX ONE -
*A Closer Look at the Vision of Hell Contained in the
First Part of the Secret of Fatima* 87

APPENDIX TWO -
Penance, Martyrdom and the Third Part of the Secret of Fatima ... 93

APPENDIX THREE -
The Miracle of the Sun and the Secret of Fatima 97

APPENDIX FOUR -
The Rosary and the Secret of Fatima 103

NOTES 113

The 'Third Secret of Fatima Vision' Artwork 115

The Third Secret of Fatima

*A*fter the two parts which I have already explained, at the left of Our Lady and a little above, we saw an Angel with a flaming sword in his left hand; flashing, it gave out flames that looked as though they would set the world on fire; but they died out in contact with the splendour that Our Lady radiated towards him from her right hand: pointing to the earth with his right hand, the Angel cried out in a loud voice: 'Penance, Penance, Penance!'.

And we saw in an immense light that is God: 'something similar to how people appear in a mirror when they pass in front of it' a Bishop dressed in White 'we had the impression that it was the Holy Father'. Other Bishops, Priests, men and women Religious going up a steep mountain, at the top of which there was a big Cross of rough-hewn trunks as of a cork-tree with the bark; before reaching there the Holy Father passed through a big city half in ruins and half trembling with halting step, afflicted with pain and sorrow, he prayed for the souls of the corpses he met on his way; having reached the top of the mountain, on his knees at the foot of the big Cross he was killed by a group of soldiers who fired bullets and arrows at him, and in the same way there died one after another the other Bishops, Priests, men and women Religious, and various lay people of different ranks and positions.

Beneath the two arms of the Cross there were two Angels each with a crystal aspersorium in his hand, in which they gathered up the blood of the Martyrs and with it sprinkled the souls that were making their way to God.

— Tuy, Spain
3-1-1944

The 'Third Part' of the Secret of Fatima was written down by Sister Lucia Dos Santos on January 3, 1944 and released by the Catholic Church to the world on June 26, 2000.

FOREWORD

A CLOSER LOOK AT THE SECRET OF FATIMA
by Michael Fontecchio

While there have been hundreds of books written on the subject of Fatima, perhaps none of them approach the contents of the full Secret of Fatima more appropriately than Dr. Petrisko's newest work.

In this book, the author is certain to make clear that the story of Fatima begins long before the apparitions of 1917 and continues today, especially now that the 'Third Part' of the Secret has been made public to the world. 'It is imperative,' says Dr. Petrisko, 'that the message of Fatima be understood in its entirety, not only in its secrets.'

Using the same popular 'reader-friendly' style, Dr. Petrisko begins by explaining two of the most basic questions one must ask about the Blessed Mother - *Why is she coming to earth* and *What message from heaven does she bring*?

The reader is then marched through a short history of Marian apparitions and messages that occurred in the nineteenth century, and foreshadowed the events that would later take place at Fatima. For, it is during this time period, that Marian 'Secrets' began to emerge and the messages that accompanied these visions would take on more of an apocalyptic tone.

After a brief historical introduction to the 1917 Fatima apparitions and prophecies, the author delves right in to the controversy surrounding the 'Third Part' of the Secret of Fatima and why it took nearly sixty years for it to be released to the world.

Another valuable resource included in this book is the complete and unedited commentary that accompanied the release of the Secret and was written by Cardinal Ratzinger, the Prefect for the Congregation for the Doctrine of the Faith. The document, entitled '*The Message of Fatima*', contains a thorough investigation of the events that took place at Fatima in 1917 and traces the path of the 'Third Part' of the Secret right up until it was released to the world on June 26, 2000. It also includes a photocopy of the original 1944 hand written text of the secret by Sr. Lucia and perhaps most importantly of all, an in-depth explanation of the role of private revelation in the Church today.

The final section of this book contains several reflections on what the 'Third Part' of the Secret might mean for our world today. Included are the themes of penance, suffering and martyrdom as well as a deeper explanation of the angel with the flaming sword, and how the present pope is mysteriously tied to this secret. Featured prominently on the cover of this book is a provoking new painting, '*The Third Secret of Fatima Vision.*' The complete story behind this inspired piece of artwork and it's making is provided by the very talented artist himself, Chris Pelicano.

Dr. Petrisko completes his writing by accenting the commentary written by Cardinal Ratzinger. Indeed, private revelation plays a very significant role in our Church today. The signs of the times indicate that our Lady is mobilizing her army to bring about a coming 'Triumph' into the world.

May the readers of this book find comfort and hope in Our Lady's words, 'In the End, My Immaculate Heart will Triumph!'

INTRODUCTION

A HISTORY OF THE FATIMA APPARITIONS

On a cool spring day in 1916, Lucy Dos Santos, age 9, and her cousins, Francisco and Jacinta Marto, age 8 and 6 respectively, took their parents' sheep to pasture in a place not far from their homes in the mountain village of Fatima, Portugal, about 90 miles north of Lisbon. It started to drizzle, and the children sought shelter in a nearby cave. Suddenly across the field, a white globe of light appeared, moving over the open space toward the cave. The three children stared in awe as they saw in the center of the light a beautiful young man in flowing white garments.

The stranger began to speak: **"Fear not, I am the Angel of Peace. Pray with me."** Kneeling on the ground, he bowed low and recited this prayer three times, with the children repeating it after him: **"O my God, I believe, I adore, I hope and I love Thee. I ask pardon for those who do not believe, do not adore, do not hope and do not love Thee."**

In mid-summer, as the children were together, the angel came again and said, **"Pray! Pray a great deal. The hearts of Jesus and Mary have merciful designs on you. Offer prayers and sacrifices continually to the Most High. Make everything you do a sacrifice, and offer it as an act of reparation for the sins by**

The three Fatima visionaries, Jacinta, Francisco and Lucia

which God is offended, and as a petition for the conversion of sinners. Bring peace to our country in this way ... I am the Guardian Angel of Portugal. Accept and bear with submission all the sufferings the Lord will send you."

The angel came again in the fall of that same year, this time bearing a golden chalice in one hand and a Host above it in the other. The amazed children noticed that drops of blood were falling from the Host into the chalice. Presently the angel left both suspended in mid-air and prostrated himself on the ground, saying this beautiful prayer: **"Most Holy Trinity - Father, Son, and Holy Spirit - I adore Thee profoundly. I offer Thee the most precious Body, Blood, Soul and Divinity of Jesus Christ, present in all the tabernacles of the world, in reparation for the outrages, sacrileges and in differences whereby He is offended. And through the infinite merits of His Most Sacred Heart and the Immaculate Heart of Mary, I beg of Thee the conversion of poor sinners."**

Such was the prelude to one of the most remarkable messages every to be given from Heaven to earth - the "peace plan" of Our Lady of Fatima.

THE LADY MORE BRILLIANT THAN THE SUN

On Sunday, May 13, 1917, slightly more than a year after the angel's first visit, the children were pasturing their flocks as usual. This time they were in a rather barren hollow, known as the Cova da Iria (Hollow of Irene), which was about a mile from their homes. It was noon of a clear, sunny day, when suddenly a flash of lightning cut the air-then another. Fearing a storm, the children quickly gathered the sheep to get them home. Their glances fell upon a small holm-oak tree directly in their path. A dazzling light hovered over the topmost branches, when-wonder of wonders - what should they behold but the form of a lovely lady standing atop the tree in the light, her feet hidden in a shimmering cloud. She was like the angel, only far more beautiful. She wore a long white dress, and the mantle over her head and shoulders reaching to her feet was edged in burnished gold. Her hands were joined before her breast, and from the right hand hung an exquisite Rosary of white pearls. As Lucy later described her, "She was a lady more brilliant than the sun."

After telling the children not to be frightened, the vision said: **I come from Heaven. I want you to come here at this same hour on the 13th day of each month until October. Then I will tell you who I am and what I want."** She also told them to say the Rosary every day and to bear all the sufferings **God** would send them.

In June, the Lady appeared again. There were about 70 people present, though only the children could see the apparition. She told the youngsters that many souls go to Hell because they have no one to pray and make sacrifices for them. She said Francisco and Jacinta would soon leave the world for Heaven. Holding out her heart surrounded by thorns which pierced it from all sides, Our Lady told Lucy: **"God wishes you to remain in the world for some time because He wants to use you to establish in the world the devotion to my Immaculate Heart. I promises salvation to those who embrace it, and their souls will be loved by God as flowers placed by myself to adorn His throne."**

THE CHILDREN SEE HELL

During her appearance in July, Our Lady**,** in answer to **Lucy's** plea, promised that in October she would work a great public miracle so that all might believe and know who she was. Again the Mother of God told the children to sacrifice themselves for sinners and to say many times, especially when making a sacrifice, this prayer: **"O my Jesus, I offer this for love of Thee, for the conversion of poor sinners, and in reparation for all the sins committed against the Immaculate Heart of Mary."**

As she spoke these words, Our Lady stretched out her hands, and bright rays came forth which seemed to penetrate into the earth. All at once the ground vanished, and the children found themselves standing on the brink of a sea of fire. As they peered into this dreadful place, the terrified youngsters saw huge numbers of devils and damned souls. The devils resembled hideous black animals, each filling the air with despairing shrieks. The damned souls were in their human bodies and seemed to be brown in color, tumbling about constantly in the flames and screaming with terror. All were on fire within and without their bodies, and neither the devils nor the damned souls seemed able to control their movements. They were tossing about in the flames like fiery coals in a furnace. There was never an instant's peace or freedom from pain.

Looking with compassion at the pale and trembling little ones, the vision spoke to them: **"You have seen Hell, where the souls of poor sinners go. To save them, God wishes to establish in the world the devotion to my Immaculate Heart. If people do what I tell you, many souls will be saved and there will be peace."**

THE VISION FORETELLS WORLD WAR II AND COMMUNISM

"The war [First World War, then raging] is going to end. But if people do not stop offending God, another and worse one will begin in the reign of Pius XI. When you shall see a night illuminated by an unknown light [January 25, 1938], know that this is the great sign that God gives you that He is going to punish the world for its many crimes by means of war, hunger, and persecution of the Church and the Holy Father."

"To prevent this, I shall come to ask for the conversion of Russia to my Immaculate Heart and the Communion of Reparation on the five first Saturdays. If my requests are granted, Russia will be converted and there will be peace. If not, she will scatter her errors throughout the world, provoking wars and persecution of the Church. The good will be martyred, the Holy Father will have much to suffer, and various nations will be destroyed..."

"...But in the end, my Immaculate Heart will triumph, the Holy Father will consecrate Russia to me, Russia will be converted, and a certain period of peace will be granted to the world."

The Lady asked that this message be kept secret until she gave permission to reveal it.

THE CHILDREN ARE JAILED

The apparitions rapidly were creating so much excitement that the atheistic civil authorities became alarmed. At the next scheduled appearance of the vision, August 13th, though more than 15,000 people were waiting in the Cova, the atheistic mayor of Ourem, under whose jurisdiction Fatima belonged, had the children kidnaped and place in jail. In spite of his threats to have them burnt alive in boiling oil, the children refused to reveal the secret given to them. Fearing violence from the people, the mayor released Lucy and her cousins the next day. Near the village of Valinhos on August 19th, the Lady appeared to the children again. She told them she was greatly displeased by the action of the mayor. As a result, the miracle promised for October would not be as great as originally planned.

More than 30,000 people were present in September, and saw a shower of mysterious white petals fall to within 10 feet of the ground before dissolving into the air. Many also saw the globe of light bearing the Lady come to rest atop the tree, and the branches bend as though someone were standing on them. Later, they saw the cloud depart into the east, from whence it had come.

70,000 GATHER FOR THE PROMISED MIRACLE

By now, all Portugal was stirred by the events taking place at Fatima, suddenly the most important spot in the land. Particularly were the newspapers interested, especially in the statement that a great miracle was to take place. Many reporters and photographers were on hand to record the events, or to prove that the statements were nothing more than lies.

On the day preceding October 13th, all roads led to Fatima, with people coming from all parts of the land in any form of transportation they could find. Many walked for miles over the rough fields. It rained all the night of the 12th and the morning of the 13th. By noon, more than 70,000 had crowded into the Cova. Standing in the mud up to their ankles, they huddled together under umbrellas, seeking protection from the relentless rain as they prayed their Rosaries.

Shortly after noon the Lady arrived for her final appearance. She told the children:

"I am the Lady of the Rosary. I have come to warn the faithful to amend their lives and to ask pardon for their sins. They must not offend Our Lord any more, for He is already too grievously offended by the sins of men. People must say the Rosary. Let them continue saying it every day."

THE SUN WHIRLS IN THE SKY

As the Lady was about to leave, she pointed to the sun. Lucy excitedly repeated the gesture, and the people looked into the sky. The rain had ceased, the clouds parted, and the sun shone forth, but not in its usual brilliance. Instead, it appeared like a silver disc, pale as the moon, at which all could gaze without straining their eyes. Suddenly, impelled by some mysterious force, the disc began to whirl in the sky, casting off great shafts of multicolored light. Red, green, blue, yellow, violet - the enormous rays shot across the sky at all angles, lighting up the entire countryside for many miles around, but particularly the upturned faces of those 70,000 spell bound people. After three minutes, the wonder stopped, but was resumed again a second and a third time - three times in all - within about 12 minutes. It seemed that the whole world was on fire, with the sun spinning at a greater speed each time.

Then a gasp of terror rose from the crowd, for the sun seemed to tear itself from the heavens and come crashing down upon the horrified multitude. **"It's the end of the world!"** shrieked one woman. **"Dear God, don't let me die in my sins!"** implored another. **"Holy Virgin, protect us!"** cried a third. All were on their knees in terror, asking pardon for their sins. Just when it seemed that the ball of fire would fall upon and destroy them, the miracle ceased and the sun resumed its normal place in the sky, shining forth as peacefully as ever.

When the people arose from the ground, cries of astonishment were heard on all sides. Their clothes,

Witnessing the Miracle of the Sun at Fatima, October 13, 1917

which had been soaking wet and muddy, now were clean and dry. Many of the sick and crippled had been cured of their afflictions.

THE CHILDREN ENJOY SPECIAL VISIONS

While the miracle of the sun was taking place, the children alone were privileged to witness several remarkable visions in the heavens. As Our Lady had promised, St. Joseph had come with the Holy Family and he had blessed the world. Then, Our Lady appeared as the Mother of Sorrows, accompanied by her Divine Son, who also blessed the world. Finally, Lucy had seen the Blessed Virgin Mary, dressed in brown robes of Our Lady of Mount Carmel, crowned as Queen of Heaven and Earth, holding a brown Scapular in her hand, with her infant Son upon her knee. However, in none of these visions had any of the figures spoken to the children.

Truly, it had been a great day for Portugal. The reporters, many of whom had come to scoff, gave long and detailed accounts of what had taken place, while the newspapers published many photographs of the great crowds and of the children. Although these were released to the entire world (copies are on file in the U.S. Congressional Library), few people outside Portugal paid any attention to these events, and newspapers in most other countries ignored the story completely.

PART II SUBSEQUENT IMPORTANT EVENTS

As the Blessed Mother had promised, Francisco and Jacinta soon joined her in Heaven. The little boy died from the flu in April, 1919, and his sister from pleurisy in February, 1920.

Before she died, little Jacinta revealed some little known but remarkable statements made by Our Lady of Fatima. Here are some of them:

> "More souls go to Hell because of sins of the flesh than for any other reason."
> "Certain fashions will be introduced that will offend Our Lord very much."
> "Many marriages are not good; they do not please Our Lord and are not of God."

"Priests must be pure, very pure. They should not busy themselves with anything except what concerns the Church and souls. The disobedience of priests to their superiors and to the Holy Father is very displeasing to Our Lord."

"The Blessed Mother can no longer restrain the hand of her Divine Son from striking the world with just punishment for its many crimes."

"If the government of a country leaves the Church in peace and gives liberty to our Holy Religion, it will be blessed by God."

"Tell everybody that God gives grace through the Immaculate Heart of Mary. Tell them to ask graces from her, and that the Heart of Jesus wishes to be venerated together with the Immaculate Heart of Mary. Ask them to plead for peace from the Immaculate Heart of Mary, for the Lord has confided the peace of the world to her."

OUR LADY APPEARS WITH THE CHRIST CHILD TO SISTER LUCIA

In 1921, upon the advice of the Bishop of Leiria - Fatima, Lucy entered a convent boarding school to learn to read and write. Later she became a nun in the order, a Sister of St. Dorothy, whose mother house was at Tuy, Spain.

One day, while Lucy (now, Sister Lucia) was kneeling in prayer in the convent chapel (December 10, 1025), the Blessed Mother and the Christ Child appeared to her with a new and wonderful message for souls. The first to speak was the Christ Child, who said **"Have pity on the heart of Your Most Holy Mother. It is covered with thorns with which ungrateful men pierce it at every moment, and there is no one to remove them with an act of reparation."**

Holding in her hand a heart encircled with sharp thorns, Our Lady then said to Sister Lucia: **"My child, behold my heart surrounded** with the thorns which ungrateful men place therein at every moment by their blasphemies and ingratitude. You at least try to console me. Announce in my name that I promise to assist at the hour of death with all the graces necessary for salvation, all those who, on the first Saturday of five consecutive months, go to Confession and receive Holy Communion, recite the Rosary, and keep my company for a quarter of an hour while meditating on the mysteries of the Rosary, with the intention of making reparation to me."

SISTER LUCIA'S SECRET

Our Lord appeared to Sister Lucia in 1927, this time giving her permission to reveal the first two parts of the message of Fatima: 1) the vision of Hell, including the promise to take the children to Heaven, the predictions of another war, martyrdom for Christians, the destruction of nations, the persecution of the Church and of the Holy Father, and the spread of Communism. 2) The devotion to the Immaculate Heart of Mary. All this had previously been kept a secret.

In 1929, Our Lady came once again. She completed the promise made on July 13th to come and ask for the consecration of Russia to the Immaculate Heart of Mary and the Communion of Reparation of the First Saturdays.

"The moment has come in which God asks the Holy Father, in union with all the bishops of the world, to make the consecration of Russia to my Immaculate Heart, promising to save it by this means. There are so many souls whom the Justice of God condemns for sins committed against me, that I have come to ask reparation: sacrifice yourself for this intention and pray."

If men would fulfill her requests, Russia would be converted and there would be peace.

Of course there was still the unknown part of the message of Fatima that was not revealed until 2000. Prior to 1950, Sister Lucia wrote down this secret and placed it in an envelope which was sealed and given to the Bishop of Fatima to be opened in 1960.

[Editor's Note: In 1960 the letter was opened, and its contents were read by Pope John XXIII. At that time, ecclesiastical authority decided not to reveal it to the general public. No one in authority had ever said the secret would be revealed to the world, but only that the letter would be opened in 1960.] (See article on pages 4&5.) On the night of January 25, 1938, Sister Lucia stood at her convent window and saw an ominous red glow that lit the entire sky. This light was seen throughout Europe and Africa and in part of America and Asia. Scientists tried to explain it as a Aurora Borealis, or Northern Lights. But Sister Lucia knew that it was the great sign foretold by Our Lady on July 13, 1917, and that the punishment of the world was at hand. Several weeks later, Hitler invaded Austria striking the match that was to set the world aflame. Thus began another and worse war in the reign of Pius XI as predicted by the Mother of God at Fatima. [This article was originally published in *Our Lady Queen of Peace Vol.* II, December 1992. The majority of this article was excerpted with permission from the book *Our Lady of Fatima's Peace Plan for Heaven*, published by *Tan Books and Publishers*, Rockford, Illinois.]

CHAPTER ONE

WHY DOES MARY APPEAR?

Two thousand years ago, Scripture tells us that God the Father sent His only begotten Son, Jesus, to redeem us—His children—from the bondage of sin and death. Scripture tells us that Christ is the Way, the Truth, and the Life—sent by God to lead us back home to Him. After Jesus' death, resurrection, and ascension into heaven, God sent His Holy Spirit to purify and refine us so that Presence could dwell in us. But for this to happen, we clearly needed to cooperate with His Grace.

So to aid us in this effort, He sent Mary, the Queen of Prophets, the Queen of Heaven, the Queen of Peace. She was not only the Mother of Jesus, the Mother of God—but she was also our Mother, given to all mankind at the foot of the cross.

If we look closely at the Christian era, we will see that Mary, our Mother, has been actively involved with God's children, her children, for a purpose—to return us to our heavenly Father. This is done, the Church teaches, not only through her role in our redemption, in mediating God's graces, and by serving as our advocate before God, but Mary also has a longstanding history of mystical interaction with her earthly children.

Indeed, Marian apparitions and supernatural manifestations have been reported since the earliest days of the Church. They have paralleled, in an almost complimentary fashion, the spiritual, social, and political needs of God's children. And Church history is filled with such stories.

Beginning in A.D. 40, just seven years after the death of Christ, Mary reportedly appeared to St. James on the plains of northern Spain at a place named "Saragozza." Just seven years later, she is said to have appeared again to a woman named Villa at Le Puy, France. After this, the rest is more than history. Throughout every century, in every land, there are stories of Mary coming from heaven to the aid of her children, often at the most desperate of times and in the most critical situations.

Since the Middle Ages there have been many efforts to gather such reports of Mary's appearances. Many books have been written, including some very well written accounts that solidify and enhance the overall history of Marian interventions. But over the last fifty years, a series of scholarly studies have documented this phenomenon which have elevated the field of mystical theology to a new level. Especially noted is Robert Ernst's 1989 work titled *Lexikon der Marienerscheinungen*, which studied not only apparitions and visions but such phenomena as weeping and bleeding images, and was a look at all the reported apparitions he could uncover since the beginning of the Church. Although his work has been criticized, it also has been noted as a useful tool in charting the relative frequency and increase in the number of reported apparitions over the centuries. Ernst found that reports of Marian apparitions began to multiply significantly during the tenth century (except for a slight decline in the 14th century). He also found the 20th century alone (400 in his study) equaled the total number from all of the preceding centuries. This, of course, did not include the present decade (1990's) which continues to reveal more reports. A similar effort, *Les Apparitions de la Vierge*, was published by Sylvie Barnay for his doctoral dissertation in 1992. Barnay's study noted data from 2460 texts on apparitions.

Another highly referenced work is Fr. Bernard Billets 1971 study *True and False Apparitions in the Church*. This study found 210 apparitions reported between 1928 and 1971. A revised study published in 1976 continued to document the escalating number of reports. C.M. Staehlin wrote in his book *Apparitions*, that there were 30 apparitions of Mary "investigated" in Western Europe between 1930 and 1950, with some 300 cases of individual apparitions to children. And Yves Chiron's 1997 study *Enqu^te Sur Les Apparitions De La Vierge* reported over 300 twentieth century apparitions. Another study by W.A. Christian Jr., titled *Religious Apparitions and the Cold War in Southern Europe*, estimated as many as fourteen apparitions a year were reported to Catholic officials in the 1940's and 1950's in Europe.

While these studies are in no way considered by their authors to be precise, they do verify estimates and shed greater light on the entire field of modern day apparitions. It is a field that is mysterious in many ways, but one that is growing in interest especially among secular scholars and investigative writers. Some very accomplished scholars have published books on the subject over the last two decades, as have many professional lay Catholics who have developed strong interest in the field. In his 1998 book, *The Last Secret,* investigative journalist Michael Brown continued to reveal the vastness of this field of mystical theology. Brown writes that officials at the International Research Institute at the University of Dayton told him that at least eight thousand significant apparitions of the Virgin Mary have occurred since the earliest centuries. Father Johann G. Roten, director of the institute, estimated close to a thousand major, minor, and related apparitions have occurred between 1830 and 1981. Two other works, *A Guide to Apparitions of Our Blessed Virgin Mary* (1995) by Peter Heintz and *Erscheinungen und Botschaften der Gottesmutter Maria* (1995) by Gottfried Hierzenberger and Otto Nedomansky, also confirm the uniqueness of our times and the vast amount of interest in the subject by laymen.

Indeed, these studies document and confirm the apparitional woman's role in salvation history. But besides providing documented evidence of mystical phenomena over the centuries, the studies reveal something more. According to their authors, a documentable "outbreak" of Marian apparitions is discernible. This outbreak did not begin in the 20th century or even around 1830, the year many theologians note as the "official" onset of the Marian era because of the apparitions at Ru Du Bac, Paris. Rather, a careful examination of the past three centuries uncovers a more precise picture of the increasing phenomena of Marian apparitions.

From newspaper archives, as well as Church documents throughout Europe over the last 250 years, a wealth of data on reported apparitions emerges. Conclusions are difficult to make, but beginning somewhere in the mid to late 18th century, a trend of such reports began and continued throughout the 19th and 20th centuries.

The non-Catholic literature on Marian apparitions during the earliest part of this period is small but helpful. It consists mostly of local newspaper reports of the events and editorial commentaries. In some cases, major newspapers in larger cities became interested in the events and published stories. Often written in hostile language that was unsympathetic and agnostic, the reports paid little attention to the visionaries or their revelations but rather emphasized details of the events and the political and commercial interests served by the visions. Many newspaper accounts also explored the events in a style that sought to propagate the emerging psychological and philosophical movements of the day. For the most part, these accounts attributed the events to certain "afflicted types" or to the political, religious, and social aspirations of estranged groups during this period.

But beyond attempts by the secular press to marginalize the events in their reader's minds, another picture of the reported apparitions of this period can be found in these accounts. These events were considered great dramas, especially throughout Europe, and they drew millions of people to distant valleys and lofty mountains where the Virgin Mary was believed to be appearing. Likewise, according to historians, the apparitions were a tremendous source of religious revival and were clearly counterproductive to the emerging social and political movements of the day. Indeed, hostile government officials throughout Europe consistently blamed the Catholic Church for orchestrating many of the events.

From the Church's standpoint, except for the great increase in the number of alleged apparitions, there was nothing different about the nature of the reports. The 19th century Marian apparitions were consistent with such accounts documented as far back as the 4th and 5th centuries. According to historians, by the 11th century the phenomena of Marian apparitions was well known. By then, studies of apparitions had been published and "classic" cases were already recognizable. Reports of such events continued throughout the late Middle Ages with documents revealing how accounts of visions contributed to the inception of shrines, pilgrimages, and stories of miracles.

However, immediately before the French Revolution (1789) a sharp increase in the number of Marian apparitions were reported. Some stereotypical changes occurred too, as records indicate more children and female visionaries. There is also a noted shift in the cults surrounding the events. The emphasis of such events seemed to move from being centered around the visionaries, as in the 15th and 16th centuries, to the reported "prophetic" messages the apparitions were giving to their messengers. But beginning around 1780, records show that there was an outbreak of miracles and that a growing number of priests, nuns, monks, and lay people began to prophesy about coming revolutions, wars, apostasy, droughts, food shortages, and persecution of the Church.

Indeed, from across Europe, the stories came from everywhere. Visions, miracles, prophecies, Eucharistic miracles, celestial signs, moving and weeping statues, and the stigmata were claimed in France, Germany, and the Papal States. Over the next hundred years, an endless stream of such phenomenon was reported. From the "Winking Madonnas" of Italy in the 1790's to the apparitions reported by a group of school children at Tilly-Sur-Seulles in the Calvados in 1896-99, an amazing picture of the late 18th and 19th centuries emerges. It is a picture that immediately sends a distinct message to believers of such affairs. God was trying to give the faithful a message. And His determination to do so was to be so visible and persistent as to be undeniable.

Most of all, these prophecies did what prophecies have always done, they helped secure for believers tangible proof of God's existence and that God was concerned with the world and its cooperation with His Will. While opponents voiced numerous objections to these events at the time, the evidence reveals the prophecies were not for or against any political regime. Rather, they were surprisingly indifferent for the most part. Noted Notre Dame historian Thomas Kselman explores this in his book *Miracles and Prophecies In Nineteenth Century France*:

> The eighteenth century prophecies were not part of a reasoned argument intended to refute Enlightenment deism or atheism. Rather, they spoke directly to the emotions and satisfied the spiritual needs of the people who required not simply that God exists, but that He exists as a personality who could directly communicate His desires and plans to His followers.

Kselman also noted that whether the prophecy called forth opposition to the regime or attempted to support it, the function remained the same. The prophecies insisted that the "political order align itself with the supernatural order, and strive for the creation of a godly Kingdom of Earth."

Of course, the times at hand looked little like a striving for such a kingdom. And for the faithful, the prophecies only helped to confirm that something evil was in the air and that God was warning of danger.

According to Professor David Blackbourn of Harvard University, "the total number of alleged (19th century) apparitions ran to many hundreds." This estimate, arrived at by a secular scholar through research for his book on an 1876 apparition of the Virgin Mary in the German village of Marpingin, casts a bright light on the true history of 19th century apparitions. Blackbourn's work is helpful in looking at this emerging phenomena and its vastness. But with most of the reported miracles of the 19th century, the background information today is scant. However, we must remember that there is no denying these events occurred and that they tremendously influenced the times.

Throughout the world, apparitions were increasingly being reported. Again, the prophecies were often of a warning nature and seemed to be saying a climax in world history of some sort was approaching.

At Fatima in 1917, which the Church recognized in 1930, an impressive number of prophecies were given and later fulfilled. Most significantly, the apparitional woman spoke of an era of peace that was to come into the world. However, the prophecies also said that a great purging of evil would be necessary if her attempts to call the world to conversion failed. Over the next 80 years, a new level of genocide in human history was recorded as the message of the prophets was ignored, rejected and even ridiculed.

Over decades, the world has witnessed what appears to be the approaching fulfillment of Fatima's remaining prophecies. Hundreds, if not thousands of apparitions have been reported. The end of an era is hurtling towards us, the prophets say. The errors of humanism, of what began with the French Revolution, are about to fall. Likewise, it is prophesied that a new dawn will now come into the world as the story of an age of evil passes by.

CHAPTER TWO

THE PHENOMENON OF MARIAN SECRETS

In Scripture, the idea of divine secrets is prefigured in St. Paul's epistle to the Ephesians when he speaks of God's "secret" plans.

Theologians say that Mary's secrets exist in the same context because they involve what St. Paul declared to be "the Mystery of Christ."

Theologian and Mariologist Fr. Joseph Pelletier, A.A., comments on the nature of these mysterious secrets: "The word, 'secret,' has a magical effect on people. It arouses curiosity and stimulates interest. God makes use of this to draw attention to the message he wishes to transmit through his heavenly messenger."

While this may be true, Fr. Slavko Barbaric, OFM, says we must benefit from the secrets or Mary wouldn't give them.

"It is certain for us that the secrets also contain impetus for us," Fr. Barbaric said, "The messages tell us what we have to know for now. The fact of secrets is found again and again in Marian apparitions; obviously they belong to the educational method of the Blessed Mother, which trains one to patience and an ability to wait. We must wait for much until the time for it has come."

Theologian Fr. Réne Laurentin says it is apparent Mary gives secrets to her visionaries because the times are urgent and the future is threatened:

> The secrets then have one function. They motivate the urgency for conversion. Their general theme is well-known. The world has peacefully abandoned itself to sin.

It has wanted to live joyfully, 'freely,' without God, without faith or love. New-look prophets have announced the death of God, the death of the Father, as good news; and sexual freedom among other things, as good news, but also freedom of the passions and human impulses of violence. The world is destroying itself. It is vehemently preparing its own destruction for having struggled, forgotten, or relegated the essential: God and His law of love ... The secrets announce, to a large extent, the imminent destructions which are not extrinsic punishments, but imminent justice, the self-destruction of a world which entrusts itself to evil through deviation and frenzy.

But perhaps it is in the simple words of Sr. Lucia of Fatima who wrote in her memoirs that we can find the most profound reason why God used secrets in the life of Mary herself:

> In spite of my good will to be obedient, I trust Your Excellency will permit me to withhold certain matters concerning myself as well as Jacinta, that I would not wish to be read before I enter eternity. You will not find it strange that I should reserve for eternity certain secrets and other matters. After all, is it not the Blessed Virgin herself who sets me the example? Does not the Holy Gospel tell us that Mary kept all things in her heart? And who better than this Immaculate Heart could have revealed to us the secrets of Divine Mercy? Nonetheless, she kept them to herself as in a garden enclosed, and took them with her to the palace of the Divine King.

For the most part, many of the secrets are said to deal with God's plans for His people. But before we try to comprehend some of this, it is important to understand how these secret messages began in the apparitions of the Blessed Virgin Mary. Because from their history, we can better understand their significance.

While Mary has been reportedly appearing since Zaragoza, Spain, in the 1st century, it was not until the 19th century at Rue du Bac, Paris, that the mystery of her secret messages began to unfold. This is where it all started, say theologians. St. Catherine Laboure revealed she had been given secrets, "several things I must not tell."

St. Catherine's revelation is the starting point for this mystery of secrets. But it was with the approved apparitions of the Blessed Virgin Mary at La Salette in 1846 that this element of the Virgin's revelations emerges as a point of significant interest; not just to the faithful, but to the Church hierarchy investigating the apparition.

Indeed, once the presence of secrets at La Salette were known, public speculation about their content and nature became rampant. Everyone wanted to know if the "special knowledge" concerned them in any way, and if so, what could be done to escape harm. At La Salette, public figures, institutions, different interest groups, members of religious orders, clerics, bishops, cardinals, and even the pope became involved in a drama surrounding the secrets that stretched all the way into the 20th century.

All of this began when the two visionaries, Melanie Calvat and Maximin Gerard, reported that when the Blessed Virgin Mary spoke to them on September 19, 1846, she gave each of them a secret message.

At first, the children apparently made no reference to the secrets in their accounts of the apparition. But upon repeated interrogations during the first week, from September 21-26, Maxamin and then Melanie revealed that personal "secrets" were confided to them. In a letter dated October 12, 1846, Abbe Melin, Cure of Corps, addressed a letter to Victor Rabillou, a librarian at Bourgoin, that briefly noted the existence of the secrets. This was the first document to cite the presence of the secrets. But at this point, the secrets were considered to be of a personal, not public, nature.

The earliest written account of the apparition in mid-October 1846 also disclosed the secrets. This was from the notes of Abbe Louis Perrin, the newly appointed Cure of La Salette, who interviewed the children. According to available documentation, the children initially refrained from even speaking of the secrets for fear of revealing them. But once they were known to exist, an almost ceaseless effort began by an array of investigators to dislodge them. Over time, the children repeatedly outmaneuvered their interrogators, but this did nothing to

The two LaSalette visionaries, Maximin Gerard and Melanie Calvat

inhibit the efforts. Threats of punishment and death, bribes, tricks, and pretense all failed to get the children to reveal the secrets. On the positive side, their determination was seen as evidence of their integrity and, therefore, increased the probability that the apparition was authentic.

As the months went by, the pressure on the children continued. When asked if the secrets concerned Heaven, Hell, the world, religion or other matters, Melanie replied, "It concerns that which it concerns; if I tell you this you will know it, and I don't want to tell it."

In the spring of 1847, a report written by Dr. Armand Dumanoir, a Grenoble lawyer, revealed for the first time the possibility the children's secrets were of public relevance. "After these words," wrote Dumanoir, "the Lady gave to each of them a secret which appears to consist in the announcement of a great event, fortunate for some, unfortunate for others."

With this document, a new stage in the mystery of Marian apparitions was upon the world. Church officials now began to intensify their investigation process. The public also started to voice its interest, especially since there was great social and political turmoil in France in 1848. Many began to speculate that the children's secrets were vital for understanding the unfolding contemporary events.

At this time, Church officials also began to write letters of inquiry to the priests involved with the children. By 1849, rumors were running amok, with the contents of the secrets at the center of them. Various scenarios were being outlined, with even "the second coming of Christ" foretold to be at the culmination. Rumors involving Catherine Laboure and then an actual visit by Maximin to the Cure of Ars, Jean Vianney, all contributed to efforts designed to have the children reveal their secrets. But Melanie and Maximin would not budge.

Finally, in June of 1851, Pope Pius IX was informed that the children were willing to transmit their secrets to him. The Pope agreed to the arrangement. On July 2nd Maximin sat down and recorded his secret. Upon finishing, he reportedly sat up and threw the paper in the air, declaring, "I am unburdened. I no longer have a secret. I am as others! One no longer has any need to ask me anything. One can ask the Pope and he will speak if he wants."

On July 3rd, the next day, Melanie wrote down her secret. Claiming she forgot to write something, she repeated the action on July 6th. The children said that they finally agreed to tell the secrets because they now understood the position of the Pope within the Church. But further information disclosed that both children believed they were graced with special "signs" from heaven that permitted the disclosures.

The secrets of LaSalette were then given to Pope Pius IX on July 18, 1851. The Pope opened and read them in the presence of the Grenoble officials. Ironically, this series of events, which finally brought the secrets into the hands of the Pope, also exacerbated speculation that the secrets were apocalyptical in content. Reports and rumors about the audience the conveyors of the secrets had with the Pope further fueled this speculation. Likewise, other reports from a handful of clerics who read the secrets began to emerge. Altogether, the public began to piece together a picture that fit in with their apocalyptic suspicions.

Some of the information was factual. Witnesses who observed the children write their secrets reported the children's facial expressions and other aspects of their behavior. One witness noted that Melanie asked how to spell "Antichrist." The length of the texts were noted, as was which of the two secrets was longer.

In addition, Pope Pius IX's reaction upon reading the secrets seemed to convey more information. According to the representatives present, the Pope stated upon reading Maximin's message, "Here is all the candor and simplicity of a child." However, upon reading Melanie's secret, the witnesses said that the Pope's face changed and reflected strong emotion. When he finished, he reportedly stated, "It is necessary that I reread these at more leisure. There are scourges that menace France, but Germany, Italy, all Europe is culpable and merits chastisement. I have less to fear from open impiety, than from indifference and from human respect. It is not without reason that the Church is called militant and you see here the captain."

Afterwards, further comments were attributed to the Pope by respected sources. Cardinal Lambruscini, first minister to Pius IX and Prefect of the Congregation of Rites, reportedly said, "I have known the fact of La Salette for a long time and as a Bishop I believe it. I have preached it in my diocese and I have observed that my discourse made a great impression. Moreover, I know the Secret of LaSalette."

Cardinal Fornaric, Nuncio to Paris, said, "I am terrified of these prodigies; we have everything that is needed in our religion for the conversion of sinners, and when Heaven employs such means, the evil must be very great."

Upon returning home from Rome, Abbe Gerin told Melanie

that he did not know what she had written, but judging by the Pope's reaction, it wasn't flattering. He then asked Melanie if she knew what the word "flattering" meant. Melanie replied "to give pleasure" and then she added, "But this (the secret) ought to give pleasure to the Pope - a Pope should love to suffer."

Year's later, Father Geraud reportedly stated that in a later audience with Pope Pius IX the Holy Father responded to an inquiry much in the same manner that some contemporary Church leaders have responded today when asked about the third part of the Secret of Fatima. Pope Pius said, "You want to know the secrets of La Salette? Ah, well here are the secrets of La Salette: if you do not do penance, you will all perish."

While the apparitions of the Virgin Mary at LaSalette received full approval of the Church, the secrets did not. However, the contents of the secrets continued to be circulated, with eventually Melanie herself releasing a version. This version of Melanie Calvat's secret message is actually what is known today as the Secret of LaSalette. This is because Melanie's long secret message contained the apocalyptic references only, not Maximin's. As the years went by, the secrets became irrevocably present in the public realm and this knowledge convinced many Catholics that to know the contents of the secrets of La Salette was crucial to an understanding of the critical times in which they lived. Of course, the teaching authority of the Church established itself as the official guardian of the secrets, and as time went by, the Church moved to silence all versions of the secrets by issuing official Church decrees ordering the faithful to "refrain from treating and discussing the matter under any form." The last decree came in 1923, more than seventy-five years after the apparition at La Salette. But to this day, the secrets still circulate among the faithful.

Most significantly, with the secrets of LaSalette, the drama of such prophetic information was permanently introduced into the difficult spectra of understanding the purpose of a reported apparition and its revelations. Why would God choose to reveal something, and then move to inhibit its circulation? Thus, with La Salette a whole new era in Marian prophecy is begun. And besides the confidential aspects of some of the revelation, we also find the elevation of the roles of the visionaries to new heights and mystery.

The Church also now found itself in a most uncomfortable situation after LaSalette. While wanting to reap the fruits of authentic events, the presence of secrets placed its very trustworthiness on the line and caused Church officials to be torn between understanding the public's desire to know and its mission to protect sound doctrine from contamination and confusion.

CHAPTER THREE

NINETEENTH CENTURY VISIONS OF MARY

Not long before Fatima, reports of Marian apparitions began to mount. With them, Mary reportedly brought messages that began to prepare the way for her powerful revelations at Fatima in 1917. In 1880, Mary reportedly appeared to an Anglican monk in Lanthony, South Whales, and in Blaine, France, a stigmatist named Marie-Juli Jahenny began to attract considerable attention throughout the continent. Jahenny's detailed visions of fire falling from the sky and holocaust scenarios are still cited today. Because of her credibility as a suffering victim, her Book of Revelation- type prophecies were well noted and stood out at the time. In Rouigo, Italy, in 1883, a seventeen year-old seamstress named Maria Inglese said Mary appeared to her in her room. In what may be considered a direct link to her later requests at Fatima, Maria said the Virgin requested **"atonement communion on the first Saturday's of the month."**

    A year later, the Virgin reportedly appeared as the Queen of the Rosary on March 3, 1884, to Fortuna Agrelli. Mary told Fortuna she would heal her grief if she prayed a "Rosary Novena." The girl was indeed healed on May 8th of that year. During the same month and year (March 1884), Mary appeared in the French Alps to Marie-Louise Nerbollier at Lyon and at Diemoz, France. The Virgin again recommended the Rosary and reportedly confirmed to Marie that she had appeared at La Salette. Marie Nerbollier received the stigmata and in 1939 her body was discovered to be incorrupt. Another apparition was reported in 1884 at Montligeon where again the Madonna came as the Sorrowful Mother, this time requesting prayers for the poor souls in Purgatory.

This entire period witnessed many foreshadowing elements of Fatima. Repeatedly, Mary was seen as the Sorrowful Mother, one of the ways she appeared in the sky to the visionaries at Fatima on October 13, 1917. There were also many requests to pray the Rosary and for acts of reparation, key elements of Fatima's message. It is especially noted how during this period Pope Leo XIII elevated the Rosary to the forefront of the Church and the family. He penned 12 Apostolic letters on the Rosary and transformed it from a mere popular prayer to what it is today—the spiritual weapon so many Church leaders and Mary herself say will eventually bring the collapse of evil. During the last apparition at Fatima, Mary announced she was the **"Lady of the Rosary."**

In 1886, two girls at St. Pierre-Eynac France, Francoise Prade, and Marie Grousson, reported 19 apparitions of Mary from July through November, 1886. The girls said the Virgin often wore a black veil and that they saw a cross overturned in the background of the vision, a reminder of her prophecies at Rue du Bac to St. Catherine Laboure. At Castelpetroso, Italy, on March 22, 1888, two country women looking for sheep reported seeing the Virgin Mary again as the Sorrowful Mother. Although doubts grew, so did the number of witnesses. Eventually, over a thousand people said they saw Mary and many healings were reported. Finally, on September 26, 1888, the bishop himself said that he saw the Virgin Mary three times. Pope John Paul II went on pilgrimage to Castelpetroso on March 19, 1995.

At Vallensanges France, Mary appeared 20 times in a clover field to a 13 year-old girl named Jean Bernhard. The apparition occurred from July 19 through September 29, 1888. The Virgin reportedly wept for "the sins of mankind and the coming justice." Several miracles confirmed the apparitions as Jean said Mary appeared in a "blinding white robe." Around the same time, the Virgin Mary appeared independently to three French Canadians in 1888 at the Church of Cap de la Madeleine in Quebec on the St. Lawrence River. A shrine commemorating the visions is still there today, and like Castelpetroso, was visited by Pope John Paul II.

During the early 1890s, the tidal wave of miracles continued. There were apparitions and a bleeding statue reported at Campocavallo, which the Church acknowledged, and at Sigy, France on August 5, 1890, where the Virgin reportedly appeared to two children named Alfred and Marie Cailleaux. Similar to Fatima, Mary was reported to come in a luminous cloud, with a long veil held by angels. The angels were silent but the children reported hearing a wonderful song being sung. In 1894, another 12 year-old girl reported that Mary appeared to her in Szezk-Bita, Poland. The girl's name was Julian Pezda and to this day a church sits on the site. Salesian priests from Auschwitz take care of the shrine. Around the same time at Luca, Italy, a young and beautiful girl named Gemma Calgani became the recipient of apparitions, visions, and the stigmata. Gemma was later declared a saint by the Catholic Church and is greatly admired because of the fact that despite her beauty she chose God over the world. In Flanders, a statue wept in 1893-94 and a Benedictine priest there named Father Paul of Moll reported apparitions of Jesus, Mary, and the poor souls. His story is still widely circulated today. During this period, a nun named Sister Louise Margaret Claret de la Touche began receiving revelations of Christ's Infinite Love in a convent at Romans in the south of France. To this day, her revelations are also circulated among the faithful.

From 1896 through 1899, in the French village of Tilly-sur-Suelles in the Calvados, a 14 year-old shepherdess named Louise Poliniere and group of children reported apparitions of the Virgin Mary. At Tilly-sur-Suelles, the Virgin appeared to the children as they gazed out of their classroom windows across a field some twelve hundred yards away. In the distance, the youngsters said they could see an oval of a brilliant light containing the figure of Our Lady of the Miraculous Medal. The apparitions were also seen by dozens of nuns who taught at the school. Once more, Mary invited her onlookers to pray the Rosary and to do penance. Powerful visions of a coming judgement were reportedly given at Tilly-Sur-Suelles and signs in the heavens and a solar miracle were witnessed by many. There were also demonic influences.

In 1898, apparitions were reported at Aschaffenberg, near Frankfort in Germany. The visionary, Barbara Weigand reportedly received visions of Jesus, Mary, and many saints. The revelations called for frequent reception of the Eucharist and revealed that "hard times" were coming. In May of that same year, the Virgin reportedly told Barbara that what was shaping up in the world and what could be expected as the 20th century dawned on the horizon. **"It is quite a bad time,"** Mary told Barbara. **"Mankind stands trembling in fully anxious expectation before the days of the future."** At Loretteville, Canada, that same year, a deathly ill girl reported a vision. She was then instantly healed. While at Campitello, Corsica, in 1899, two children, Cellesia Passi (14) and Perpetua Lorenzi (13) said that Mary appeared to them dressed in white with a blue veil. Later appearances were seen by many children and adults. At Corsica, the Virgin reportedly warned the people to pray **"so that you do not go to Hell."**

Ironically, perhaps the most supernatural event of the 19th century was really not very supernatural at all at the time. In Alencon, France, a girl named Marie Francoise Thérèse Martin was born on January 2, 1873. She was raised in a home of comfort and surrounded by refinements which should have spoiled her, but through suffering and a supreme confidence in God, Thérèse Martin rapidly progressed toward sanctity. At fifteen she entered a Carmelite convent at Lisieux, France, where before she died she penned her spiritual classic *Story of a Soul*. The little book quickly revealed her formula for sanctity, permitting all who read it to understand that the call to sainthood was readily available through all walks of life, even the most humblest and hidden. Thérèse Martin died at the age of 24 on September 30, 1897, and was canonized by Pope Pius XI on May 17, 1925. "The Little Flower" revealed only one supernatural experience in her life, unlike the many visionaries in this narrative, but the fact that 100 years after her death over 2,000 churches throughout the world have adopted her name indicates that she was and remains perhaps the greatest supernatural force of the age.

Most significantly, by the early 1880's an almost universal apocalyptical theme had emerged from the apparitions, transcending most of the warnings associated with the local political upheavals and European clashes of the late 18th and the early half of the 19th centuries. More and more, the reported apparitions spoke of a danger that was approaching the whole world. Like the Secret of La Salette, which appeared to be in harmony with the more dire prophecies held in Scripture, revelation after revelation disclosed that a titanic, decisive struggle between good and evil would emerge. But the Secret of La Salette was literally terrifying. Great tribulations were announced to be coming, as its contents disclosed that Hell would now to be opened, and that wars, nature, and apostasy would come to shake the world:

> **"God will strike in an unprecedented way. Woe to inhabitants of the earth! God will exhaust His wrath upon them, and no one will be able to escape so many afflictions together... . God will allow the old serpent to cause divisions among**

those who reign in every society and in every family... .Justice will be trampled underfoot and only homicides, hate, jealousy, lies, and dissension will be seen without love for country or family.... Physical and moral agonies will be suffered. God will abandon mankind to itself... .Churches will be locked up or desecrated... .A great number of priests and members of religious order will break away from the true religion... .There will be bloody wars and famines, plagues and infectious diseases... .Lucifer, together with a large number of demons, will be unloosed from hell... They will put an end to faith little by little... nature is asking for vengeance... .The earth will be struck by calamities of all kinds... .The seasons will be altered... .A general war will follow which will be appalling. For a time, God will cease to remember France and Italy because the Gospel of Jesus Christ has been forgotten. All the civil governments will have one and the same plan, which will be to abolish and do away with every religious principle, to make way for materialism, atheism, occultism, and vice of all kinds."

Many similar prophecies of a great spiritual war emerging are discernable from the records of the reported revelations during this period. Mirjam Banardy of Israel stated in 1858 that Mary had told her of "increased demonic activity" and how "Satan was growing in power." In Italy, in the early 1850's, a priest from Turin named Don Bosco reported powerful dreams that even the Pope recognized as having importance. Bosco's dreams seemed to read the future of Italy, France, Rome and Paris. Some of them, such as *the Two Columns*, were believed to be incredibly prophetic of the "end times."

In Ars, France, a saintly little priest named John Vianney, known as the Cure of Ars, reported a demonic infestation of verifiable proportion. Thousands were flocking to Ars during the 1850's to be confessed by the little priest and the dark side revealed its rage. "The devil has a very ugly voice," said Vianney. But he added that "one gets used to everything."

The Cure's fellow priests insinuated to him that it was a figment of his imagination. "It's in your head that plays you tricks," one of them remarked. But just one night in Ars always brought swift retractions. As the priests would rush into his room terrified, they would often find the good Cure resting peacefully. With a smile he would remark, "I am sorry, I forgot to warn you beforehand. However, it is a good sign: there will be big fish tomorrow."

In 1866, a nun in the Congregation of the Daughters of Mary in Anglet claimed that Mary showed her a vision of demons let loose on the earth wreaking devastation. While largely unnoticed, the Bishop of Bayonne supported her revelations and ordered printed a half-million copies of a prayer she said Mary gave her to combat the evil spirits. Was this a forerunner to Pope Leo XIII's prayer to St. Michael the Archangel, which reportedly originated from a vision the Holy Father experienced on October 13, 1884?

Leo XIII's own mystical experiences reportedly included his overhearing of a conversation between God and Satan that disclosed the unleashing of Hell and a coming era in which God's people would be put to the test. Likewise, at Pellovoison, France, where the Bishop approved the apparitions, the devil again figured prominently. Estelle Faguette's messages revealed dire warnings of evil **"conquering"** the world. Soon would come, Mary told Estelle, **"a time of trials."** The same kind of apocalyptic message was heard at Medelsheim in 1873, where the children said the Virgin warned of a great **"bloodbath."**

The Church would especially come to feel the brunt of evil's invigorated campaign, the seers said. Indeed, another curious prophecy of the time emerges to bear witness to the truth of what the visionaries were saying. "In my time the devil is outside the Church," said John Henry Cardinal Newman (d. 1890). In about one hundred years, the devil will be inside." (Mary's Church-approved message at Akita, Japan, in 1973 fulfilled Cardinal Newman's prophecy: **"The devil will infiltrate even into the Church in such a way that one will see cardinals opposing cardinals, bishops against bishops. The priests who venerate me will be scorned and opposed by their conferees... churches and altars will be sacked, and the Church will be full of those who accept compromises. The demon will press many priests and consecrated souls to leave the service of the Lord."**

Blackbourn noted in his study, upon review of an 1883 apparition at Hartervald, Germany, involving an adolescent visionary named Elisa Recktenwald, that "there is an apocalyptic tone here that exceeds anything to be found in 1876-77." (Elisa Recktenwald reported apparitions in which Mary bemoaned the "suffering and unrepentant" world. Mary reportedly said to Elisa, **"Have I not appeared already to so many of my children? Yet so few have believed."** The local bishop moved to discipline the child as well as the parents.)

Kselman recorded a similar observation concerning the rise in prophecy in his book *Miracles and Prophecies in Nineteeth Century France*:

> "The popularity of prophecy in the early years of the Third Republic is evident in the increased attention given to it in the press and by the Church, and in the number of prophetic works published. The production of prophetic books and pamphlets increased more then fivefold in the decade 1870-1879 as compared to the previous ten years. Msgr. Dupanloup, in a decree of 1874, critical of the literature, related the popular interest in prophecy to the same political crisis referred to by Remond [a renowned 19th century social historian]: *Everywhere there is talk only of miracles and prophecies, and to our generation one can say what Our Lord said to His: "This generation looks for a sign, Generatio ista signum quaerit." (Mark 8:12)"*

But not all the prophets emerging during this period were delivering revelations of woe. Some were predicting the dawn of a new era of peace and love for the world. One voice during this time specifically noted such a coming time. Luisa Picarreta (1865-1947), who became known as the Little daughter of the Divine Will, was a stigmatist from Corato, Italy, and was confined to her bed for 64 years. Reportedly a mystic of the highest order, her revelations comprised many volumes and declared a new era of grace was coming. It would begin, she said, after the earth was purged at the turn of the millennium. Most of all, this new era of Divine Will would see, Picarreta wrote, the coming of the Kingdom of the Father. The Church is presently investigating her revelations and moving towards declaring her a saint.

As noted, the total number of reported apparitions in the 19th

century ran into the hundreds. More were reported in France and Italy, but there were reports from around the world. Little can be learned about most of them because writers have concentrated on the Church-approved ones, which, in turn, resulted in inferior documentation on the unapproved ones. However, unless one dismisses it all, there is plenty of evidence to conclude that something unique occurred during the 19th century leading up to Fatima that had never occurred before and which continues to this day.

A tidal wave of miracles and prophecies deluged the world, warning of an exponentially growing danger that would cause great suffering, bloodshed, and death for the human race. No one can say how many of these reports were actually true. (There were reportedly as many 65 false visionairies at Lourdes after the onset of the apparitions in 1858.) But considering their visible merit and the hostile political times at hand, one should not be surprised if many of these cases are not reopened in the future after the age of rationalism has evaporated. Indeed, many of the apparitions deserve a just verdict that is void of the political pressures and intimidation that existed almost everywhere throughout the 19th century.

However, the greatest signs of authenticity for many of the prophets and prophecies were the events that unfolded over the century. Whether a devout atheist or a devout believer, who can deny that by the end of the 19th century, the fulfillment of many of the revelations of the 18th century was discernable to a great degree. William A. Christian, Jr., noted that by the end of the 19th century even the Vatican realized the many apparitions could not be ignored. And although few were approved, a change in policy was to its advantage. Christian explains this shift in Vatican policy:

> "Toward the end of the nineteenth century, however, when Catholicism was on the defensive, the Vatican came to realize that the Church should play to its strength. In southern Europe that strength lay in localized religion. By "crowning" Marian shrine images, the papacy associated them with the universal Church. Rome also endorsed a new series of proclamations of Marian images as patrons of dioceses or provinces. *And it regarded with increasing sympathy visions of Mary that led to the establishment of new shrines.* For by the nineteenth century virtually every adult in the Western world knew

that there were profoundly different ways to organize society and imagine what happened after death. The industrialization of Europe in the eighteenth century had separated large numbers of rural folk from local authority and belief and many migrants to cities had found alternatives to established religion in deism, spiritism, science, or the idea of progress.

"The continued strength of Catholicism in nineteenth-century France was an incentive for intellectuals to challenge the idea of the supernatural radically and intensively. As a result, French Catholics needed all the divine help they could get. Throughout the century they sought and received innumerable signs that God and, in particular, the Virgin Mary were with them. An efficient railway system and press ensured that regional devotions could reach national audiences. *Secularization was a global problem, and the Vatican developed a global response to centralize and standardize devotion.* France and Italy served as laboratories for devotional vaccines against moral diseases. Religious orders distributed these vaccines. Indeed, Our Lady of Lourdes became a new kind of general devotion, one with its origin in the laity. Replicas of the image entered parish churches worldwide."

Statistical documentation of the many millions who died during the wars and political upheavals of the 19th century would certainly be the most impressive confimation of the great turmoil prophesied and then fulfilled during this period. History clearly reveals the fall of the monarchies and the Papal States and the rise of modern socialism, which would lead to atheistic communism. The roots of so many other philosophical and political movements of this period that today hold great influence are also clearly discernable and, therefore, easily correlative to the prophecies of the 19th century. These range from the occult to communism, from materialism to sensualism, feminism to radical atheism. The 19th century saw the beginnings of so many modern day evils that many books are readily available for anyone seeking to research it all. But perhaps the greatest and most tangible evidence of the mounting danger the apparitions warned of is the evolution of weapons and warfare during this period. Moreover, the progress mankind made in its ability to wage war from the French Revolution to the early 20th century is stunning.

Indeed, the age of modern warfare had arrived and the changes were sweeping. Field guns undid fortresses. Artillery capability changed land and sea battles. Improved roads and canals made armies more mobile and the innovation of conscription, which requisitioned men by law, brought into existence armies that were reminiscent of the hordes of barbarians in the ancient world. By the mid-19th century some governments were mobilizing the youth of both sexes which brought whole nations in step with the military. Large battles were waged. In 1813 at Leipzeg, 539,000 fought. At Solferino in 1859, 300,000 men fought in a battle that ranged over sixty square miles. Before 1861, the U.S. army was 16,000. By the end of the Civil War the South had called up 90% of its men (approximately 1,400,000) and the North 45% (2,900,000).

The technological innovations of warfare were continuous during the 19th century. Rifle accuracy went from 100 yards to 1,000 yards. Bullets became cylindrical in shape and revolvers and pistols were now mass produced. By the 1860's, some companies were making 1,000 rifles a week. Soon, rapid fire guns were developed and by 1900 machine guns could massacre infantrymen. In South Africa, machine guns were used for the first time that fired 2,000 rounds in three minutes.

Artillery had its own critical development. Large shells could now rip apart wooden ships causing the development of armored ships, wagons, and trains. Inventions such as land and sea-mines, torpedoes, and stream-driven battle ships further added to the science of killing.

The technological and organizational preparations for modern warfare seemed to be preparing the world for what some politicians feared to be approaching—a great war. This would be one that industry and government together could advance beyond anything ever before seen. One in which a nation could come to believe—because of its industrial-military capabilities—that it could wage to grab "world power," and maybe even more, "world control." But if not careful, as the American Civil War statesman Henry Adams observed, the rapid advance in military capability was also previewing a more dire possibility—the danger of "world destruction." And it was this idea that seemed to dominate the message Mary would continue to bring in her 20th century apparitions, especially in her plea at Fatima.

CHAPTER FOUR

THE FATIMA PROPHECIES

The early 20th century brought no reprieve from reports of the supernatural. Again, as in the 19th century, there were waves of apparitions before and during political upheavals. Likewise, growing numbers of visionaries reported that the Virgin Mary was warning of "mounting evil" and an approaching "storm."

In 1900, Mary was seen by several people in Luca, Italy and by crowds in Tung Lu and Peking, China. That same year, two women in Tanganika, Africa said Mary appeared to them. In 1901, a 4 year-old girl from Eppelborn reported an apparition of the Virgin Mary and a woman named Elizabeth Catez (better known as Elizabeth of the Trinity) entered the Carnel of Dijon, France, where she would reveal profound mystical writings on the Holy Trinity. In 1902, a woman in Esphesus named Helen said Mary appeared to her at Panama Kapulu, the house reportedly where Mary and St. John the Evangelist lived. In 1904, a teen age boy in Zdunska-Wola, Poland, said he received an apparition. In 1905, a Eucharistic miracle occurred on the French island of Reunion in the Indian Ocean. Several thousand people witnessed the face of Christ on a host. The miracle attracted world-wide attention. On April 20, 1906, dozens reported seeing a weeping Madonna at a boarding school in Quito, Ecuador. In 1907, in the village of Porlow, County Waterford, Ireland, a child known as Little Nelly of God attracted a stir. Nelly was said to experience ecstasies, utter prophetic statements and to be able to survive on just Holy Communion.

In France and Belgium, many new reports of miracles were made. At Angers, a nun named Sister Gertrude Marie reported visions in 1907 of a coming triumph of the Church and a great number of "saints to be."

In Chambery, a sister of the Order of the Visitation named Mary Martha Chambon (d.1907) claimed that Jesus appeared to her and asked for a devotion to His Holy wounds. Christ also asked that sufferings be offered, she noted, for the "sins of the world." In Bordeaux, beginning in 1909, a woman named Marie Mesmin reported apparitions of Mary and messages that concerned the need for more prayer and a looming chastisement for "the world's sins." While in 1910 at Brussels, Belgium, a woman named Berthe Petit began having visions and apparitions. Berthe received the stigmata and prophesied two years in advance that the heir to the Austro-Hungarian empire would be killed. She also prophesied WWI and WWII. A year later, Brussels was the site of another apparition. Around the same time, detailed prophecies of "world wars" were given by a French priest at Le Pailley named Father Lamy.

At Foggio, Italy, another stigmatist, Francesco Forgione, known later to the world as Padre Pio, emerged at this time. Like other mystics, Padre Pio saw a world headed for ruin. Pio had many mystical gifts including prophecy, reading souls and bilocation. He also reportedly foretold the rise of Pope John Paul II to the papacy. Over 100,000 people attended Padre Pio's funeral on September 23, 1968. It was a fitting tribute to a saintly man and mystic who reported so many unique qualities, such as bilocation, celestial perfume, reading souls, remarkable conversions, and prophetic insight. He remains to this day the most famous mystic of the 20th century. After World War I, around 1920, Padre Pio foretold that the League of Nations wouldn't survive and that a second world war would come. "I predicted that the League of Nations wouldn't last," he reminded a friend. "These nations are going to tear each other to pieces." By the time of World War II, his statements on the course of events were well known for their accuracy. Padre Pio saw that Germany's June 22, 1941, invasion of Russia would be rebuked ("Can a fly swallow an elephant?") and that Italy and its ally, Germany would be destroyed. "You can tell Mussolini," said Pio after messengers from the Italian dictator came to see him in 1943, "that nothing can save Italy now!"

Not long before World War I, Mary appeared to a crowd of approximately 500 in Alzonne, France. Again, she warned of war. During this same period, there were a series of apparitions reported in Germany and Austria. In the Ukraine, Mary appeared at Hrushiv in 1914 to 22 people. The prophecies were dark as Mary foretold decades of suffering to come for the Ukrainian people. (Under Joseph Stalin, an estimated 10 million Ukrainians were murdered or deliberately starved to death. Millions more perished during World War II and after.)

During World War I there were more reports of apparitions. One of the most intriguing was at LaMaine, France. At LaMaine, Mary appeared to German troops from September 5 to 12, 1914. Because of the visions the Germans reportedly stopped their attack. Afterwards, soldiers were ordered under penalty of death to never repeat what they had seen. Of course World War I did nothing to deter belief in all the mystics, visionaries, and prophecies. Such a violent war had never before occurred and by its end an estimated 12 million lay dead, thereby fulfilling in the minds of many the numerous 19th century prophecies of the coming of "great wars and much bloodshed." There were other apparitions reported during World War I. In 1917, Mary was reportedly seen in Paris, Moscow, and Barral, Portugal. A year later, three children in Mazillac, France, claimed they saw the Virgin. But of course the most famous were the apparitions at Fatima.

Without question, theologians tell us that the apparitions at Fatima in 1917 solidified Heaven's more than century-long conversation with the world. First appearing on May 13, 1917, Mary told three shepherd children the 20th century was moving rapidly forward toward an unpleasant date with its destiny, and that mankind was flirting with **"annihilation."** But if people changed, she added, it would hasten an **"era of peace."** Mary also promised to return to ask for the consecration of Russia and the Communion of Reparation on the first Saturdays. The Church was rather favorable from the beginning, as Pope Benedict XV wrote to the bishops of Portugal one year after the apparitions saying that he considered them "an extra ordinary favor from God." Fatima was a great call to conversion and was, perhaps more than any apparition in Church history, characterized by a series of prophecies that were fulfilled.

At Fatima, Mary foretold the following:

1) **The October 13, 1917, great sign (the miracle of the spinning and falling sun) witnessed by an estimated 70,000 people.**
2) **The rise of an evil (communism) out of Russia.**
3) **A great sign on a night that lights up the sky. (This occurred on January 25- 26, 1938, when a bright light over the northern hemisphere illuminated the night and**

was witnessed by millions. Scientists said it was an aurora borealis but according to the lone surviving visionary of Fatima [Lucia dos Santos], it was the promised sign that would occur before the outbreak of the second world war which began a little more than a month later when Hitler took over Austria. Eight months later Germany invaded Czechoslovakia. Some note that this date is also the day on the Church calender that commemorates the conversion of St. Paul. Paul, as Scripture details, was confronted suddenly by a great light in the sky that flashed down upon him.)

5) Persecution of the faithful and especially the Holy Father.
6) The end of World War I.
7) A second great war.
8) Russia will scatter her errors throughout the world, provoking wars. (The Korean and Vietnam wars were Russian agitated as were the wars in several African nations, Afghanistan, El Salvador and Nicaragua. Numerous internal civil conflicts throughout the world can also be linked to Russia.
9) God was going to punish the world by means of further wars, hunger and persecution
10) Various nations will be annihilated.
11) Portugal would always keep the faith. (By this statement, some Fatima scholars have suggested that other parts of the world would not keep the faith and, therefore, a great apostasy was being prophesied to come.)
12) An era of peace.

A few lesser known prophecies of Fatima can also be confirmed as having been fulfilled. Mary said the second world war would break out under the reign of Pius XI, which it did, and that Jacinta Marto and Francisco Marto, the two youngest Fatima visionaries, were soon going to heaven. Both died within several years of the apparitions. (Francisco died in Fatima on April 4, 1919 while Jacinta passed away in a Lisbon hospital on February 20, 1920.) The prophecies of Fatima took decades to fulfill and most were not really known until the early 1940's. At that time, portions of the memoirs (five separate works, the last of which was published in Portuguese in March, 1990) of Sister Mary Lucia dos Santos, the lone surviving Fatima visionary and a nun of the Sisters of St. Dorothy, began to be released. But it is in what occurred one month after the apparitions at Fatima ended that the profound importance of Fatima is revealed and understood.

On July 13th, 1917, Mary spoke of the need for the conversion and consecration of Russia. The Bolshevik Revolution was still 6 months away when the three shepherd children at Fatima thought the Virgin's words concerning Russia that day were in reference to a person, not a nation. But time would quickly reveal the extraordinary reality of Mary's words to the three shepherd children. In November 1917, just one month after the October 13th apparition and "Miracle of the Sun" at Fatima, the Bolshevik communist Party seized power through a revolution in Russia. Led by Nikolai Lenin, the party replaced the ruling Romanoff family and set out to organize a world revolution based upon the communist Manifesto of Marx and Engels of 1848. This philosophy advocated seizure of power by the proletariat and the establishment of a transitional socialist state, with state control of labor, industry, distribution, and credit. Co-operation was not voluntary but mandatory and all classes of people had to be assimilated.

The philosophical concepts of modern communism actually stem from Sir Thomas More's 1516 work *Utopia* and 18th century French philosophers Rousseau, Robespierre, and Saint-Just. The conspiracy of Francois Baleuf in 1796 was intended to establish this system during the French Revolution but fell short. The Russian revolution was, however, financially sprung by the same secret societies that had fostered the French Revolution and that had been condemned by so many popes. Pope Leo XIII foresaw this evil approaching when he warned in his 1884 encyclical *Humanum Genus* that a danger brewed that intended to undermine the existing order of the world, and that the secret societies were behind it.

"Tear away the mask of Freemasonry," Leo wrote, "and make it plain to all what it is. It aims at the utter overthrow of the whole religious order of the world which Christian teaching has produced and the substitution of a new state of things—based on the principles of pure naturalism. Including almost every nation in its grasp, it unites itself with other sects of which it is the real inspiration and the hidden motive-power."

Marxist-Leninism embraced this same purpose, but to an even greater extent. It declared war on three fundamental institutions: the family, religion, and on the ownership of private property. Massive brutality, torture, and death came with the Bolshevick revolution in Russia, and in a short period of time it became evident that the driving force behind communism was a profound, spiritual, literally demonic hatred for God and religion. (Historians note that Marx, Lenin, Trotsky, Engels Stalin and Mao were spiritualists. Several were Satanists. Stalin, Marx, and Engels were Illuminati [secret society] recruits.) Tens of thousands of churches were closed and millions were imprisoned or murdered for their beliefs.

Over the decades, it also became apparent that Russia, because of its atheistic, militaristic principles, was becoming the threat it was foretold to be at Fatima: **"she** (Russia) **will spread her errors throughout the world provoking wars and persecution of the Church."** By the 1950's, the Soviet Union, which included Russia, was aggressively pursuing its worldwide communist agenda. And because of its weapons of mass destruction, Mary's unfulfilled prophecy of the annihilation of nations now lingered over the world, suspended day to day for decades in what became a tug of war between the forces of good and evil, both visible and invisible.

Likewise, fire raining from the heavens was believed to have been symbolically represented in the great Fatima signs of both 1917 and 1938. Mary's last image in the sky at Fatima on October 13th, as Our Lady of Mt. Carmel, did nothing to diminish this understanding. This is because Mary's title of Our Lady of Mt. Carmel is related to the prophet Elias, who lived on Mt. Carmel and reportedly foresaw Mary in a vision centuries before her life on earth, and is most known for the miracle in which he called down fire from the sky, a fire that not only consumed the sacrifice but also the water in the trench around it. The vision of Our Lady of Mt. Carmel occurred at Fatima on October 13th just as the sun appeared to be falling from the sky. Then, as with Elias, immediately after the miracle the ground was dry as were the people's clothes. The Feast of Our Lady of Mt. Carmel is July 16th and it was that day, the following year, that proved to be the last full day of life for the last Tsar of Russia, Nicholas II and his family. The Romanoffs were executed by the communists on July 17th, 1918. (On July 17, 1998, the 80th anniversary date of their murder, the Romanoff family was buried in an official ceremony in St. Petersburg. The Vatican's Moscow-based ambassador to Russia, Archbishop Bukovsky attended the Orthodox burial service.) Twenty-seven years later, on July 16, 1945, fire did somewhat rain down from the heavens as the first atomic explosion was detonated at the Trinity site in New Mexico.

CHAPTER FIVE

THE CONTROVERSIAL 'THIRD PART' OF THE SECRET

Pope Pius XII, without any public declaration, responded to the request of Our Lady of Fatima when he consecrated the world to her Immaculate Heart on Fatima's silver jubilee in 1942. Pope John XXIII is known to have read the Third Secret and made a decision to keep its contents hidden.

Pope Paul VI in his apostolic exhortation *Signum Magnum* directed the world to the message of Fatima and to Mary as its "Great Sign." And Pope John Paul II has kept the message of Fatima at the forefront of his pontificate in both word and deed.

Thus, the message of Fatima is truly the best source for what so many visionaries are predicting. Fatima's words, while not as extensive or as detailed as many contemporary private revelations, still represents the essence of almost all 20th century prophecies.

Indeed, if there is ever a great wall in the Vatican covered with paintings depicting the 20th century Church approved Marian apparitions, those representing Beaurang, Banneux and Akita, would be displayed prominently on this wall. But Fatima would *be* the wall. In Mary's message at Fatima we can detect where Pope John Paul II and others have taken their direction. Fatima tells us much.

On Sunday, May 13, 1917, Mary first appeared to the three children. After calming their fears, the Virgin said: **"I come from Heaven. I want you to come here at this same hour on the thirteenth day of each month until October. Then, I will tell you who I am and what I want."**

In June, Mary came again on the 13th. After revealing to the children that **"Francisco and Jacinta would soon leave the world for Heaven,"** the Virgin told Lucia, **"God wishes you to remain in the world for some time because He wants to use you to establish in the world the devotion to my Immaculate Heart. I promise salvation to those who embrace it, and their souls will be loved by God as flowers placed by myself to adorn His throne."**

Finally, in July, Mary gave the visionaries what has come to be known as the Secret of Fatima. Stretching out her arms, the children witnessed a beam of light penetrate into the earth, and they saw a sea of fire and a huge number of damned souls:

> **You have seen hell, where the souls of poor sinners go. To save them, God wishes to establish in the world the devotion to my Immaculate Heart. If people do what I tell you, many souls will be saved and there will be peace.**
>
> **The war [World War I] is going to end. But if people do not stop offending God, another and worse one will begin in the reign of Pius XI. When you shall see a night illuminated by an unknown light [Jan. 25, 1938], know that this is the Great Sign that God gives you that He is going to punish the world for its many crimes by means of war, hunger, and persecution of the Church and the Holy Father.**
>
> **To prevent this, I shall come to ask for the consecration of Russia to my Immaculate Heart and the Communion of Reparation on the five first Saturdays. If my requests are granted, Russia will be converted and there will be peace. If not, she will scatter her errors throughout the world, provoking wars and persecution of the Church. The good will be martyred; the Holy Father will have much to suffer, and various nations will be annihilated.**
>
> **But in the end, my Immaculate Heart will triumph, the Holy Father will consecrate Russia to me, Russia will be converted, and a certain period of peace will be granted to the world.**

The Virgin Mary then asked that this message be kept secret until she gave permission to reveal it, and it is because of this request that Fatima has gained much notoriety. Even though most of the Virgin's messages were eventually disclosed, a portion was not. This part became known as the "Third Secret of Fatima" or more correctly the "Third Part of the Secret of Fatima."

In what *was* released of the secret of July 13, 1917, we find the two most significant revelations that have been consistently reemphasized over the years in many of Mary's messages. These revelations concern the promise of an "Era of Peace," but also the harrowing reminder that before this peace comes, there may be a severe trial leading to the "annihilation of nations."

This prophecy caused great interest in the Third Secret's contents. Although repeatedly denied by some Fatima authorities, many believed the unrevealed portion contained specific details of the "annihilation."

Over the decades, the controversy surrounding the Third Secret escalated, especially since 1960 when Pope John XXIII decided to not reveal its contents. According to Sr. Lucia's memoirs, she did not write down the contents of the Third Secret until late 1943 or early 1944, and they were not necessarily intended to be revealed:

> "It may be, Your Excellency, that some people think that I should have made known all this some time ago because they consider that it would have been twice as valuable years beforehand. This would have been the case if God had willed to present me to the world as a prophetess.
>
> "But I believe that God had no such intention when He made known these things to me. If that had been the case, I think that in 1917 when He ordered me to keep silent, and this order was confirmed by those who represented Him, He would, on the contrary, have ordered me to speak. I consider then, Your Excellency, that God willed only to make use of me to remind the world that it is necessary to avoid sin, and to make reparation to an offended God by means of prayer and penance. (Sr. Lucia's memoirs, *In Her Own Words,* by John Haffert)"

Responding to concerns about Sr. Lucia's death, Bishop Correia da Silva requested her to write down the Third Secret. Afterwards, she placed the Secret in a sealed envelope and delivered it to Bishop da Silva. On December 8, 1944, the bishop placed the envelope in a larger envelope and instructed that it be given to His Eminence Cardinal Don Manuel, Patriarch of Lisbon "after my death."

While the bishop was given permission by Sr. Lucia to read the Secret's contents, he refrained from doing so because he said it had been addressed to the Holy Father. The envelope was then sent to the Apostolic Nuncio, Msgr. Cento (now Cardinal Cento), who forwarded it to the Sacred Congregation for the Doctrine of the Faith.

Although Pope Pius XII was alive at the time, he reportedly never read the Secret. His successor, Pope John XXIII, read it and reportedly stated the "text did not pertain to his times." He preferred to leave an assessment of its contents to his successors. Pope John XXIII made no public statements about the case.

At that time, it was believed the Secret was to be revealed either in 1960 or upon the death of Sr. Lucia, whichever came first. This allegation was later denied, as sources close to the Secret sought to defend Pope John XXIII's decision.

Cardinal Ottaviani, who reportedly also read the Secret, stated, "Yes, the Secret is important; it is important for the Holy Father for whom it was defined. It was addressed to him. And if the one to whom it was addressed has decided not to declare now is the moment to make it known to the world, we should be content with the fact that in his wisdom he wished it to remain a secret."

In 1963, Pope Paul VI succeeded Pope John XXIII and reportedly read the Secret. At the 50th anniversary of Fatima, he reportedly revealed his awareness of the Secret's contents:

> "The first intention is for the Church; the Church, One, Holy, Catholic and Apostolic. We want to pray, as we have said, for its internal peace. What terrible damage could be provoked by arbitrary interpretations, not authorized by the teaching of the Church, disrupting its traditional and constitutional structure, replacing the theology of the true and great Fathers of the Church with new and peculiar ideologies; interpretations intent upon stripping the norms of faith

of that which modern thought, often lacking rational judgment, does not understand and does not like. ... we want to ask of Mary, a living Church, a true Church, a united Church, a holy Church."

While Pope John Paul I met with Sr. Lucia the year before his election, there is no evidence that he had read the Secret before his death. Although it has been written in reputable publications that Sr. Lucia, in this private meeting, reportedly foretold Cardinal Allino Luciani's election to the Chair of Peter.

Pope John Paul II read the Third Secret of Fatima, and reportedly made a public comment related to its contents. In an interview from the Oct. 13, 1981 issue of *Stimme des Glaubens*, a German publication, the Holy Father discusses the issues involved in making the Secret known publically:

> "On the other hand, it should be sufficient for all Christians to know this much: If there is a message in which it is said that the oceans will flood entire sections of the earth that from one moment to the other millions of people will perish. ... there is no longer any point in really wanting to publish this secret message. ... many want to know merely out of curiosity or because of their tastes for sensationalism, but they forget that to know implies for them a responsibility."

In concluding this interview, the Pope describes future trials for mankind:

> "We must be prepared to undergo trials in the not-too-distant future, trials that will require us to be ready to give up even our lives, and a total gift of self to Christ and for Christ. Through your prayers and mine, it is possible to alleviate this tribulation, but it is only in this way that the Church can be effectively renewed. How many times, indeed, has the renewal of the Church been effected in blood?
>
> "This time, again, it will not be otherwise. We

must be strong, we must prepare ourselves, we must entrust ourselves to CHRIST and to His Holy Mother, and we must be attentive to the prayer of the Rosary."

Cardinal Ratzinger, the prefect for the Congregation of the Doctrine of the Faith, read the Secret. In his book *The Ratzinger Report*, author Vittorio Messori quotes the Cardinal as having said the Secret contains a serious warning:

> "A stern warning has been launched from that place [Fatima] that is directed against the prevailing frivolity, a summons to the seriousness of life, of history, to the perils that threaten humanity. It is that which Jesus himself recalls frequently, "unless you repent you will all perish"(Luke 13:3).
> "Conversion---Fatima fully recalls it to mind----is a constant demand of Christian life. We should already know from Revelation and also from the Marian apparitions approved by the Church in their known contents, which only reconfirm the URGENCY of penance, conversion, forgiveness, and fasting. To publish the "Third Secret" would mean exposing the Church to the danger of sensationalism, exploitation of the content."

Pope John Paul II's words and Cardinal Ratzinger's statement were intriguing since both added fuel to the debate over the contents of the Secret. The Pope and the Cardinal's words seemed to many to indicate the Secret's contents could be extremely harsh, although there were statements to the contrary.

Some noted authorities on Fatima have argued that the Secret spoke of an apostasy and nothing else. This was not to de-emphasize the seriousness of such a revelation, but to shift the focus away from apocalyptic interpretations.

In 1984, the Most Rev. Cosme de Amaral, bishop of Leira-Fatima, stated that the Secret did not concern nuclear issues but, rather, our faith:

"The Secret of Fatima speaks not about the atomic bombs, nor about nuclear warheads, not about SS-20 missiles. Its content concerns our faith. To identify the Secret with a catastrophic announcement or with a nuclear holocaust is to distort the meaning of the message. The loss of faith of a continent is worse that the annihilation of a nation, and it is true that faith is continually diminishing in Europe."

Fr. Joaquin Alonso C.M.F., the official historian of Fatima, seemed to suggest that the Secret involves a crisis in faith:

"In the period which will precede the great triumph of the Immaculate Heart of Mary, terrible things will occur, and these are the object of the Third Part of the Secret.
"What things? If in Portugal, 'the dogma of the faith will always be preserved,' it can be deduced with all clarity that in other parts of the Church these dogmas will be obscured or even lost. It is quite possible that the message not only speaks of a "crisis of faith" in the Church during this period, but also, like the Secret of La Salette, it makes concrete references to internal strife among Catholics and to the deficiencies of priests and religious. It is also possible that this may imply deficiencies even among the upper ranks of the hierarchy."

Perhaps no expert on the contents of the Secret has been quoted more than Fr. Alonso.

His statement that the Secret was not about a terrible chastisement was often referenced. However, Fatima experts note in their writings on Fatima and the meaning of its message that "Fr. Alonso does *not* rule a chastisement out."

While the emphasis on apostasy was significant, there were disclosures from other sources that indicated that part of the Secret dealt with more than the prediction of an apostasy. Something that perhaps Pope John Paul II was alluding to in the much-publicized interview with *Stimme des Glaubens* in which he hypothetically noted "millions of people will perish."

Messages to contemporary visionaries fueled the public debate over the Third Secret, its contents, and whether or not it was ever intended by Mary to be released. However, Sister Lucia was repeatedly quoted as saying the Third Secret was never meant to be released and that the popes have acted in accordance with God's Will. However, the controversy remained alive especially through the efforts of those who felt the consecration of Russia was incomplete. Some believed that the consecration of Russia was not completed exactly in accordance with Mary's original request and therefore the danger Mary warned of at Fatima still looms over the world, especially because of Russia's still prevalent nuclear arsenal. Even now that the Secret has been revealed, the issue appears to still carry some revelance in as far as to why the world is still a powder keg. Others say insufficient reparation is now the real reason, nevertheless, that by releasing the Third Secret, we now better understand the existing dangers that threaten the world with annihilation.

In the last several years, the controversy over the secret continued. On the 80th anniversary (Oct. 13, 1997) apparition of the Virgin Mary at Fatima another uproar over the Third Secret of Fatima was ignited in Rome. The periodical *Inside the Vatican* detailed the controversy in its November, 1997 issue:

> "The 80th anniversary of the last apparition of the Virgin Mary at Fatima (October 13, 1917) sparked controversy in Rome.
>
> "The issue: the famous 'Third Secret' of Fatima. The 'Third Secret' does not predict any 'cataclysmic event,' but a 'spiritual crisis,' apostasy from the faith and grave divisions in the Church the French Mariologist Father Rene Laurentin contended to Italian national television on the evening of October 12.
>
> "'The Virgin was saying: be careful, this Council will be good, but after it there will be a series of deviations and temptations,' Laurentin said. 'This is the last secret. It's too bad they have not made it public. It concerns the Church.' Pope John XXIII committed an 'error' when he decided not to publish the contents of the secret in 1960, since all of these things have come to pass since the Second Vatican Council, Laurentin added."

THEOLOGICAL COMMENTARY

THE MESSAGE OF FATIMA

Prepared by the Prefect for the Congregation for the
Doctrine of the Faith, Cardinal Joseph Ratzinger
June 26, 2000

INTRODUCTION

As the second millennium gives way to the third, Pope John Paul II has decided to publish the text of the third part of the "secret of Fatima".

The twentieth century was one of the most crucial in human history, with its tragic and cruel events culminating in the assassination attempt on the "sweet Christ on earth". Now a veil is drawn back on a series of events which make history and interpret it in depth, in a spiritual perspective alien to present-day attitudes, often tainted with rationalism.

Throughout history there have been supernatural apparitions and signs which go to the heart of human events and which, to the surprise of believers and non-believers alike, play their part in the unfolding of history. These manifestations can never contradict the content of faith, and must therefore have their focus in the core of Christ's proclamation: the Father's love which leads men and women to conversion and bestows the grace required to abandon oneself to him with filial devotion. This too is the message of Fatima which, with its urgent call to conversion and penance, draws us to the heart of the Gospel.

Fatima is undoubtedly the most prophetic of modern apparitions. The first and second parts of the "secret"—which are here published in sequence so as to complete the documentation—refer especially to the frightening vision of hell, devotion to the Immaculate Heart of Mary, the Second World War, and finally the prediction of the immense damage that Russia would do to humanity by abandoning the Christian faith and embracing Communist totalitarianism.

In 1917 no one could have imagined all this: the three pastorinhos of Fatima see, listen and remember, and Lucia, the surviving witness, commits it all to paper when ordered to do so by the Bishop of Leiria and with Our Lady's permission.

For the account of the first two parts of the "secret", which have already been published and are therefore known, we have chosen the text written by Sister Lucia in the Third Memoir of 31 August 1941; some annotations were added in the Fourth Memoir of 8 December 1941.

The third part of the "secret" was written "by order of His Excellency the Bishop of Leiria and the Most Holy Mother ..." on 3 January 1944.

There is only one manuscript, which is here reproduced photostatically. The sealed envelope was initially in the custody of the Bishop of Leiria. To ensure better protection for the "secret" the envelope was placed in the Secret Archives of the Holy Office on 4 April 1957. The Bishop of Leiria informed Sister Lucia of this.

According to the records of the Archives, the Commissary of the Holy Office, Father Pierre Paul Philippe, OP, with the agreement of Cardinal Alfredo Ottaviani, brought the envelope containing the third part of the "secret of Fatima" to Pope John XXIII on 17 August 1959. "After some hesitation", His Holiness said: "We shall wait. I shall pray. I shall let you know what I decide".(1)

In fact Pope John XXIII decided to return the sealed envelope to the Holy Office and not to reveal the third part of the "secret".

Paul VI read the contents with the Substitute, Archbishop Angelo Dell'Acqua, on 27 March 1965, and returned the envelope to the Archives of the Holy Office, deciding not to publish the text.

John Paul II, for his part, asked for the envelope containing the third part of the "secret" following the assassination attempt on 13 May 1981. On 18 July 1981 Cardinal Franjo Jeper, Prefect of the Congregation, gave two envelopes to Archbishop Eduardo Martínez Somalo, Substitute of the Secretariat of State: one white envelope, containing Sister Lucia's original text in Portuguese; the other orange, with the Italian translation of the "secret". On the following 11 August, Archbishop Martínez returned the two envelopes to the Archives of the Holy Office.(2)

As is well known, Pope John Paul II immediately thought of consecrating the world to the Immaculate Heart of Mary and he himself composed a prayer for what he called an "Act of Entrustment", which was to be celebrated in the Basilica of Saint Mary Major on 7 June 1981, the Solemnity of Pentecost, the day chosen to commemorate the 1600th anniversary of the First Council of Constantinople and the 1550th anniversary of the Council of Ephesus. Since the Pope was unable to be present, his recorded Address was broadcast. The following is the part which refers specifically to the Act of Entrustment:

> "Mother of all individuals and peoples, you know all their sufferings and hopes. In your motherly heart you feel all the struggles between good and evil, between light and darkness, that convulse the world: accept the plea which we make in the Holy Spirit directly to your heart, and embrace with the love of the Mother and Handmaid of the Lord those who most await this embrace, and also those whose act of entrustment you too await in a particular way. Take under your motherly protection the whole human family, which with affectionate love we entrust to you, O Mother. May there dawn for everyone the time of peace and freedom, the time of truth, of justice and of hope".(3)

In order to respond more fully to the requests of "Our Lady", the Holy Father desired to make more explicit during the Holy Year of the Redemption the Act of Entrustment of 7 May 1981, which had been repeated in Fatima on 13 May 1982. On 25 March 1984 in Saint Peter's Square, while recalling the fiat uttered by Mary at the Annunciation, the Holy Father, in spiritual union with the Bishops of the world, who had been "convoked" beforehand, entrusted all men and women and all peoples to the Immaculate Heart of Mary, in terms which recalled the heartfelt words spoken in 1981:

> "O Mother of all men and women, and of all peoples, you who know all their sufferings and their hopes, you who have a mother's awareness of all the struggles between good and evil, between light and darkness, which afflict the modern world, accept the cry which we, moved by the Holy Spirit, address directly to your Heart. Embrace with the love of the Mother and Handmaid of the Lord, this human world of ours, which we entrust and consecrate to you, for we are full of concern for the earthly and eternal destiny of individuals and peoples.
>
> In a special way we entrust and consecrate to you those individuals and nations which particularly need to be thus entrusted and consecrated.
>
> 'We have recourse to your protection, holy Mother of God!' Despise not our petitions in our necessities".

The Pope then continued more forcefully and with more specific references, as though commenting on the Message of Fatima in its sorrowful fulfilment:

> "Behold, as we stand before you, Mother of Christ, before your Immaculate Heart, we desire, together with the whole Church, to unite ourselves with the consecration which, for love of us, your Son made of himself to the Father: 'For their sake', he said, 'I consecrate myself that they also may be consecrated in the truth' (Jn 17:19). We wish to unite ourselves with our Redeemer in this his consecration for the world and for the human race, which, in his divine Heart, has the power to obtain pardon and to secure reparation.
>
> The power of this consecration lasts for all time and embraces all individuals, peoples and nations. It overcomes every evil that the spirit of darkness is able to awaken, and has in fact awakened in our times, in the heart of man and in his history.
>
> How deeply we feel the need for the

consecration of humanity and the world—our modern world—in union with Christ himself! For the redeeming work of Christ must be shared in by the world through the Church.

The present Year of the Redemption shows this: the special Jubilee of the whole Church.

Above all creatures, may you be blessed, you, the Handmaid of the Lord, who in the fullest way obeyed the divine call!

Hail to you, who are wholly united to the redeeming consecration of your Son!

Mother of the Church! Enlighten the People of God along the paths of faith, hope, and love! Enlighten especially the peoples whose consecration and entrustment by us you are awaiting. Help us to live in the truth of the consecration of Christ for the entire human family of the modern world.

In entrusting to you, O Mother, the world, all individuals and peoples, we also entrust to you this very consecration of the world, placing it in your motherly Heart.

Immaculate Heart! Help us to conquer the menace of evil, which so easily takes root in the hearts of the people of today, and whose immeasurable effects already weigh down upon our modern world and seem to block the paths towards the future!

From famine and war, deliver us.

From nuclear war, from incalculable self-destruction, from every kind of war, deliver us.

From sins against the life of man from its very beginning, deliver us.

From hatred and from the demeaning of the dignity of the children of God, deliver us.

From every kind of injustice in the life of society, both national and international, deliver us.

From readiness to trample on the commandments of God, deliver us.

From attempts to stifle in human hearts the very truth of God, deliver us.

From the loss of awareness of good and evil, deliver us.

From sins against the Holy Spirit, deliver us, deliver us.

Accept, O Mother of Christ, this cry laden with the sufferings of all individual human beings, laden with the sufferings of whole societies.

Help us with the power of the Holy Spirit to conquer all sin: individual sin and the 'sin of the world', sin in all its manifestations.

Let there be revealed, once more, in the history of the world the infinite saving power of the Redemption: the power of merciful Love! May it put a stop to evil! May it transform consciences! May your Immaculate Heart reveal for all the light of Hope!".(4)

Sister Lucia personally confirmed that this solemn and universal act of consecration corresponded to what Our Lady wished ("Sim, està feita, tal como Nossa Senhora a pediu, desde o dia 25 de Março de 1984": "Yes it has been done just as Our Lady asked, on 25 March 1984": Letter of 8 November 1989). Hence any further discussion or request is without basis.

In the documentation presented here four other texts have been added to the manuscripts of Sister Lucia: 1) the Holy Father's letter of 19 April 2000 to Sister Lucia; 2) an account of the conversation of 27 April 2000 with Sister Lucia; 3) the statement which the Holy Father appointed Cardinal Angelo Sodano, Secretary of State, to read on 13 May 2000; 4) the theological commentary by Cardinal Joseph Ratzinger, Prefect of the Congregation for the Doctrine of the Faith.

Sister Lucia had already given an indication for interpreting the third part of the "secret" in a letter to the Holy Father, dated 12 May 1982:

> "The third part of the secret refers to Our Lady's words:'If not [Russia] will spread her errors throughout the world, causing wars and persecutions of the Church. The good will be martyred; the Holy Father will have much to suffer; various nations will be annihilated' (13-VII-1917).
>
> The third part of the secret is a symbolic revelation, referring to this part of the Message, conditioned by whether we accept or not what the Message itself asks of us: 'If my requests are heeded, Russia will be converted, and there will be peace; if not, she will spread her errors throughout the world, etc.'.
>
> Since we did not heed this appeal of the Message, we see that it has been fulfilled, Russia has invaded the world with her errors. And if we have not yet seen the complete fulfilment of the final part of this prophecy, we are going towards it little by little with great strides. If we do not reject the path of sin, hatred, revenge, injustice, violations of the rights of the human person, immorality and violence, etc.
>
> And let us not say that it is God who is punishing us in this way; on the contrary it is people themselves who are preparing their own punishment. In his kindness God warns us and calls us to the right path, while respecting the freedom he has given us; hence people are responsible".(5)

The decision of His Holiness Pope John Paul II to make public the third part of the "secret" of Fatima brings to an end a period of history marked by tragic human lust for power and evil, yet pervaded by the merciful love of God and the watchful care of the Mother of Jesus and of the Church.

The action of God, the Lord of history, and the co-responsibility of man in the drama of his creative freedom, are the two pillars upon which human history is built.

Our Lady, who appeared at Fatima, recalls these forgotten values. She reminds us that man's future is in God, and that we are active and responsible partners in creating that future.

–Tarcisio Bertone, SDB
Archbishop Emeritus of Vercelli
Secretary of the Congregation for the Doctrine of the Faith

THE SECRET OF FATIMA

FIRST AND SECOND PARTS OF THE SECRET

According to the version presented by Sister Lucia in the 'Third Memoir' of 31 August 1941 for the Bishop of Leiria-Fatima:

> This will entail my speaking about the secret, and thus answering the first question.
>
> What is the secret? It seems to me that I can reveal it, since I already have permission from Heaven to do so. God's representatives on earth have authorized me to do this several times and in various letters, one of which, I believe, is in your keeping. This letter is from Father José Bernardo Gonçalves, and in it he advises me to write to the Holy Father, suggesting, among other things, that I should reveal the secret. I did say something about it. But in order not to make my letter too long, since I was told to keep it short, I confined myself to the essentials, leaving it to God to provide another more favourable opportunity.
>
> In my second account I have already described in detail the doubt which tormented me from 13 June until 13 July, and how it disappeared completely during the Apparition on that day.
>
> Well, the secret is made up of three distinct parts, two of which I am now going to reveal.

The first part is the vision of hell.

Our Lady showed us a great sea of fire which seemed to be under the earth. Plunged in this fire were demons and souls in human form, like transparent burning embers, all blackened or burnished bronze, floating about in the conflagration, now raised into the air by the flames that issued from within themselves together with great clouds of smoke, now falling back on every side like sparks in a huge fire, without weight or equilibrium, and amid shrieks and groans of pain and despair, which horrified us and made us tremble with fear. The demons could be distinguished by their terrifying and repulsive likeness to frightful and unknown animals, all black and transparent. This vision lasted but an instant. How can we ever be grateful enough to our kind heavenly Mother, who had already prepared us by promising, in the first Apparition, to take us to heaven. Otherwise, I think we would have died of fear and terror.

We then looked up at Our Lady, who said to us so kindly and so sadly:

"You have seen hell where the souls of poor sinners go. To save them, God wishes to establish in the world devotion to my Immaculate Heart. If what I say to you is done, many souls will be saved and there will be peace. The war is going to end: but if people do not cease offending God, a worse one will break out during the Pontificate of Pius XI. When you see a night illumined by an unknown light, know that this is the great sign given you by God that he is about to punish the world for its crimes, by means of war, famine, and persecutions of the Church and of the Holy Father. To prevent this, I shall come to ask for the consecration of Russia to my Immaculate Heart, and the Communion of reparation on the First Saturdays. If my requests are heeded, Russia will be converted, and there will be peace; if not, she will spread her errors throughout the world, causing wars and persecutions of the Church. The good will be martyred; the Holy Father will have much to suffer; various nations will be annihilated. In the end, my Immaculate Heart will triumph. The Holy Father will consecrate Russia to me, and she shall be converted, and a period of peace will be granted to the world".

"J.M.J.

The third part of the secret revealed at the Cova da Iria-Fatima, on 13 July 1917.

I write in obedience to you, my God, who command me to do so through his Excellency the Bishop of Leiria and through your Most Holy Mother and mine.

After the two parts which I have already explained, at the left of Our Lady and a little above, we saw an Angel with a flaming sword in his left hand; flashing, it gave out flames that looked as though they would set the world on fire; but they died out in contact with the splendour that Our Lady radiated towards him from her right hand: pointing to the earth with his right hand, the Angel cried out in a loud voice: 'Penance, Penance, Penance!'. And we saw in an immense light that is God: 'something similar to how people appear in a mirror when they pass in front of it' a Bishop dressed in White 'we had the impression that it was the Holy Father'. Other Bishops, Priests, men and women Religious going up a steep mountain, at the top of which there was a big Cross of rough-hewn trunks as of a cork-tree with the bark; before reaching there the Holy Father passed through a big city half in ruins and half trembling with halting step, afflicted with pain and sorrow, he prayed for the souls of the corpses he met on his way; having reached the top of the mountain, on his knees at the foot of the big Cross he was killed by a group of soldiers who fired bullets and arrows at him, and in the same way there died one after another the other Bishops, Priests, men and women Religious, and various lay people of different ranks and positions. Beneath the two arms of the Cross there were two Angels each with a crystal aspersorium in his hand, in which they gathered up the blood of the Martyrs and with it sprinkled the souls that were making their way to God.

Tuy-3-1-1944."

INTERPRETATION OF THE "SECRET"

Letter of His Holiness Pope John Paul II to Sister Lucia

To the Reverend Sister Maria Lucia of the Convent of Coimbra:

In the great joy of Easter, I greet you with the words the Risen Jesus spoke to the disciples: "Peace be with you"!

I will be happy to be able to meet you on the long-awaited day of the Beatification of Francisco and Jacinta, which, please God, I will celebrate on 13 May of this year.

Since on that day there will be time only for a brief greeting and not a conversation, I am sending His Excellency Archbishop Tarcisio Bertone, Secretary of the Congregation for the Doctrine of the Faith, to speak with you. This is the Congregation which works most closely with the Pope in defending the true Catholic faith, and which since 1957, as you know, has kept your hand-written letter containing the third part of the "secret" revealed on 13 July 1917 at Cova da Iria, Fatima.

Archbishop Bertone, accompanied by the Bishop of Leiria, His Excellency Bishop Serafim de Sousa Ferreira e Silva, will come in my name to ask certain questions about the interpretation of "the third part of the secret".

Sister Maria Lucia, you may speak openly and candidly to Archbishop Bertone, who will report your answers directly to me.

I pray fervently to the Mother of the Risen Lord for you, Reverend Sister, for the Community of Coimbra and for the whole Church. May Mary, Mother of pilgrim humanity, keep us always united to Jesus, her beloved Son and our brother, the Lord of life and glory.

With my special Apostolic Blessing.

IOANNES PAULUS PP. II

From the Vatican, 19 April 2000.

CONVERSATION WITH SISTER MARIA LUCIA OF JESUS AND THE IMMACULATE HEART

The meeting between Sister Lucia, Archbishop Tarcisio Bertone, Secretary of the Congregation for the Doctrine of the Faith, sent by the Holy Father, and Bishop Serafim de Sousa Ferreira e Silva, Bishop of Leiria-Fatima, took place on Thursday, 27 April 2000, in the Carmel of Saint Teresa in Coimbra.

Sister Lucia was lucid and at ease; she was very happy that the Holy Father was going to Fatima for the Beatification of Francisco and Jacinta, something she had looked forward to for a long time.

The Bishop of Leiria-Fatima read the autograph letter of the Holy Father, which explained the reasons for the visit. Sister Lucia felt honoured by this and reread the letter herself, contemplating it in own her hands. She said that she was prepared to answer all questions frankly.

At this point, Archbishop Bertone presented two envelopes to her: the first containing the second, which held the third part of the "secret" of Fatima. Immediately, touching it with her fingers, she said: "This is my letter", and then while reading it: "This is my writing".

The original text, in Portuguese, was read and interpreted with the help of the Bishop of Leiria-Fatima. Sister Lucia agreed with the interpretation that the third part of the "secret" was a prophetic vision, similar to those in sacred history. She repeated her conviction that the vision of Fatima concerns above all the struggle of atheistic Communism against the Church and against Christians, and describes the terrible sufferings of the victims of the faith in the twentieth century.

When asked: "Is the principal figure in the vision the Pope?", Sister Lucia replied at once that it was. She recalled that the three children were very sad about the suffering of the Pope, and that Jacinta kept saying: "Coitadinho do Santo Padre, tenho muita pena dos pecadores!" ("Poor Holy Father, I am very sad for sinners!"). Sister Lucia continued: "We did not know the name of the Pope; Our Lady did not tell us the name of the Pope; we did not know whether it was Benedict XV or Pius XII or Paul VI or John Paul II; but it was the Pope who was suffering and that made us suffer too".

As regards the passage about the Bishop dressed in white, that is, the Holy Father—as the children immediately realized during the "vision"—who is struck dead and falls to the ground, Sister Lucia was in full agreement with the Pope's claim that "it was a mother's hand that guided the bullet's path and in his throes the Pope halted at the threshold of death" (Pope John Paul II, Meditation from the Policlinico Gemelli to the Italian Bishops, 13 May 1994).

Before giving the sealed envelope containing the third part of the "secret" to the then Bishop of Leiria-Fatima, Sister Lucia wrote on the outside envelope that it could be opened only after 1960, either by the Patriarch of Lisbon or the Bishop of Leiria. Archbishop Bertone therefore asked: "Why only after 1960? Was it Our Lady who fixed that date?" Sister Lucia replied: "It was not Our Lady. I fixed the date because I had the intuition that before 1960 it would not be understood, but that only later would it be understood. Now it can be better understood. I wrote down what I saw; however it was not for me to interpret it, but for the Pope.

Finally, mention was made of the unpublished manuscript which Sister Lucia has prepared as a reply to the many letters that come from Marian devotees and from pilgrims. The work is called Os apelos da Mensagem de Fatima, and it gathers together in the style of catechesis and exhortation thoughts and reflections which express Sister Lucia's feelings and her clear and unaffected spirituality. She was asked if she would be happy to have it published, and she replied: "If the Holy Father agrees, then I am happy, otherwise I obey whatever the Holy Father decides". Sister Lucia wants to present the text for ecclesiastical approval, and she hopes that what she has written will help to guide men and women of good will along the path that leads to God, the final goal of every human longing. The conversation ends with an exchange of rosaries. Sister Lucia is given a rosary sent by the Holy Father, and she in turn offers a number of rosaries made by herself.

The meeting concludes with the blessing imparted in the name of the Holy Father.

ANNOUNCEMENT MADE BY CARDINAL ANGELO SODANO, SECRETARY OF STATE

At the end of the Mass presided over by the Holy Father at Fatima, Cardinal Angelo Sodano, the Secretary of State, made this announcement in Portuguese, which is given here in English translation:

Brothers and Sisters in the Lord!

At the conclusion of this solemn celebration, I feel bound to offer our beloved Holy Father Pope John Paul II, on behalf of all present, heartfelt good wishes for his approaching 80th Birthday and to thank him for his vital pastoral ministry for the good of all God's Holy Church; we present the heartfelt wishes of the whole Church.

On this solemn occasion of his visit to Fatima, His Holiness has directed me to make an announcement to you. As you know, the purpose of his visit to Fatima has been to beatify the two "little shepherds". Nevertheless he also wishes his pilgrimage to be a renewed gesture of gratitude to Our Lady for her protection during these years of his papacy. This protection seems also to be linked to the so-called third part of the "secret" of Fatima.

That text contains a prophetic vision similar to those found in Sacred Scripture, which do not describe photographically the details of future events, but synthesize and compress against a single background facts which extend through time in an unspecified succession and duration. As a result, the text must be interpreted in a symbolic key.

The vision of Fatima concerns above all the war waged by atheistic systems against the Church and Christians, and it describes the immense suffering endured by the witnesses of the faith in the last century of the second millennium. It is an interminable Way of the Cross led by the Popes of the twentieth century.

According to the interpretation of the "little shepherds", which was also confirmed recently by Sister Lucia, "the Bishop clothed in white" who prays for all the faithful is the Pope. As he makes his way with great difficulty towards the Cross amid the corpses of those who were martyred (Bishops, priests, men and women Religious and many lay people), he too falls to the ground, apparently dead, under a hail of gunfire.

After the assassination attempt of 13 May 1981, it appeared evident that it was "a mother's hand that guided the bullet's path", enabling "the Pope in his throes" to halt "at the threshold of death" (Pope John Paul II, Meditation from the Policlinico Gemelli to the Italian Bishops, Insegnamenti, XVII, 1 [1994], 1061). On the occasion of a visit to Rome by the then Bishop of Leiria-Fatima, the Pope decided to give him the bullet which had remained in the jeep after the asassination attempt, so that it might be kept in the shrine. By the Bishop's decision, the bullet was later set in the crown of the statue of Our Lady of Fatima.

The successive events of 1989 led, both in the Soviet Union and in a number of countries of Eastern Europe, to the fall of the Communist regimes which promoted atheism. For this too His Holiness offers heartfelt thanks to the Most Holy Virgin. In other parts of the world, however, attacks against the Church and against Christians, with the burden of suffering they bring, tragically continue. Even if the events to which the third part of the "secret" of Fatima refers now seem part of the past, Our Lady's call to conversion and penance, issued at the start of the twentieth century, remains timely and urgent today. "The Lady of the message seems to read the signs of the times—the signs of our time—with special insight... The insistent invitation of Mary Most Holy to penance is nothing but the manifestation of her maternal concern for the fate of the human family, in need of conversion and forgiveness" (Pope John Paul II, Message for the 1997 World Day of the Sick, No. 1, Insegnamenti, XIX, 2 [1996], 561).

In order that the faithful may better receive the message of Our Lady of Fatima, the Pope has charged the Congregation for the Doctrine of the Faith with making public the third part of the "secret", after the preparation of an appropriate commentary.

Brothers and sisters, let us thank Our Lady of Fatima for her protection. To her maternal intercession let us entrust the Church of the Third Millennium.

Sub tuum praesidium confugimus, Sancta Dei Genetrix! Intercede pro Ecclesia. Intercede pro Papa nostro Ioanne Paulo II. Amen.

Fatima, 13 May 2000

THEOLOGICAL COMMENTARY
BY CARDINAL JOSPEH RATZINGER

A careful reading of the text of the so-called third "secret" of Fatima, published here in its entirety long after the fact and by decision of the Holy Father, will probably prove disappointing or surprising after all the speculation it has stirred. No great mystery is revealed; nor is the future unveiled. We see the Church of the martyrs of the century which has just passed represented in a scene described in a language which is symbolic and not easy to decipher. Is this what the Mother of the Lord wished to communicate to Christianity and to humanity at a time of great difficulty and distress? Is it of any help to us at the beginning of the new millennium? Or are these only projections of the inner world of children, brought up in a climate of profound piety but shaken at the same time by the tempests which threatened their own time? How should we understand the vision? What are we to make of it?

PUBLIC REVELATION AND PRIVATE REVELATIONS – THEIR THEOLOGICAL STATUS

Before attempting an interpretation, the main lines of which can be found in the statement read by Cardinal Sodano on 13 May of this year at the end of the Mass celebrated by the Holy Father in Fatima, there is a need for some basic clarification of the way in which, according to Churc teaching, phenomena such as Fatima are to be understood within the life of faith. The teaching of the Church distinguishes between "public Revelation" and "private revelations". The two realities differ not only in degree but also in essence. The term "public Revelation" refers to the revealing action of God directed to humanity as a whole and which finds its literary expression in the two parts of the Bible: the Old and New Testaments. It is called "Revelation" because in it God gradually made himself known to men, to the point of becoming man himself, in order to draw to himself the whole world and unite it with himself through his Incarnate Son, Jesus Christ. It is not a matter therefore of intellectual communication, but of a life-giving process in which God comes to meet man. At the same time this process naturally produces data pertaining to the mind and to the understanding of the mystery of God. It is a process which involves man in his entirety and therefore reason as well, but not reason alone. Because God is one, history, which he shares with humanity, is also one. It is valid for all time, and it has reached its fulfilment in the life, death and resurrection of Jesus Christ. In Christ, God has said everything, that is, he has revealed himself completely, and therefore Revelation came to an end with the fulfilment of the mystery of Christ as enunciated in the New Testament. To explain the finality and completeness of Revelation, the Catechism of the Catholic Church quotes a text of Saint John of the Cross: "In giving us his Son, his only Word (for he possesses no other), he spoke everything to us at once in this sole Word—and he has no more to say... because what he spoke before to the prophets in parts, he has now spoken all at once by giving us the All Who is His Son. Any person questioning God or desiring some vision or revelation would be guilty not only of foolish behaviour but also of offending him, by not fixing his eyes entirely upon Christ and by living with the desire for some other novelty" (No. 65; Saint John of the Cross, The Ascent of Mount Carmel, II, 22).

Because the single Revelation of God addressed to all peoples comes to completion with Christ and the witness borne to him in the books of the New Testament, the Church is tied to this unique event of sacred history and to the word of the Bible, which guarantees and interprets it. But this does not mean that the Church can now look only to the past and that she is condemned to sterile repetition. The Catechism of the Catholic Church says in this regard: "...even if Revelation is already complete, it has not been made fully explicit; it remains for Christian faith gradually to grasp its full significance over the course of the centuries" (No. 66). The way in which the Church is bound to both the uniqueness of the event and progress in understanding it is very well illustrated in the farewell discourse of the Lord when, taking leave of his disciples, he says: "I have yet many things to say to you, but you cannot bear them now. When the Spirit of truth comes, he will guide you into all the truth; for he will not speak on his own authority... He will glorify me, for he will take what is mine and declare it to you" (Jn 16:12-14). On the one hand, the Spirit acts as a guide who discloses a knowledge previously unreachable because the premise was missing—this is the boundless breadth and depth of Christian faith. On the other hand, to be guided by the Spirit is also "to draw from" the riches of Jesus Christ himself, the inexhaustible depths of which appear in the way the Spirit leads. In this regard, the Catechism cites profound words of Pope Gregory the Great: "The sacred Scriptures grow with the one who reads them" (No. 94; Gregory the Great, Homilia in Ezechielem I, 7, 8). The Second Vatican Council notes three essential ways in which the Spirit guides in the Church, and therefore three ways in which "the word grows": through the meditation and study of the faithful, through the deep understanding which comes from spiritual experience, and through the preaching of "those who, in the succession of the episcopate, have received the sure charism of truth" (Dei Verbum, 8).

In this context, it now becomes possible to understand rightly the concept of "private revelation", which refers to all the visions and revelations which have taken place since the completion of the New Testament. This is the category to which we must assign the message of Fatima. In this respect, let us listen once again to the Catechism of the Catholic Church: "Throughout the ages, there have been so-called 'private' revelations, some of which have been recognized by the authority of the Church... It is not their role to complete Christ's definitive Revelation, but to help live more fully by it in a certain period of history" (No. 67). This clarifies two things:

1. The authority of private revelations is essentially different from that of the definitive public Revelation. The latter demands faith; in it in fact God himself speaks to us through human words and the mediation of the living community of the Church. Faith in God and in his word is different from any other human faith, trust or opinion. The certainty that it is God who is speaking gives me the assurance that I am in touch with truth itself. It gives me a certitude which is beyond verification by any human way of knowing. It is the certitude upon which I build my life and to which I entrust myself in dying.

2. Private revelation is a help to this faith, and shows its credibility precisely by leading me back to the definitive public Revelation. In this regard, Cardinal Prospero Lambertini, the future Pope Benedict XIV, says in his classic treatise, which later became normative for beatifications and canonizations:"An assent of Catholic faith is not due to revelations approved in this way; it is not even possible. These revelations seek rather an assent of human faith in keeping with the requirements of prudence, which puts them before us as probable and credible to piety". The Flemish theologian E. Dhanis, an eminent scholar in this field, states succinctly that ecclesiastical approval of a private revelation has three elements: the message contains nothing contrary to faith or morals; it is lawful to make it public; and the faithful are authorized to accept it with prudence (E. Dhanis, Sguardo su Fatima e bilancio di una discussione, in La Civiltà Cattolica 104 [1953], II, 392-406, in particular 397). Such a message can be a genuine help in understanding the Gospel and living it better at a particular moment in time; therefore it should not be disregarded. It is a help which is offered, but which one is not obliged to use.

The criterion for the truth and value of a private revelation is therefore its orientation to Christ himself. When it leads us away from him, when it becomes independent of him or even presents itself as another and better plan of salvation, more important than the Gospel, then it certainly does not come from the Holy Spirit, who guides us more deeply into the Gospel and not away from it. This does not mean that a private revelation will not offer new emphases or give rise to new devotional forms, or deepen and spread older forms. But in all of this there must be a nurturing of faith, hope and love, which are the unchanging path to salvation for everyone. We might add that private revelations often spring from popular piety and leave their stamp on it, giving it a new impulse and opening the way for new forms of it. Nor does this exclude that they will have an effect even on the liturgy, as we see for instance in the feasts of Corpus Christi and of the Sacred Heart of Jesus. From one point of view, the relationship between Revelation and private revelations appears in the relationship between the liturgy and popular piety: the liturgy is the criterion, it is the living form of the Church as a whole, fed directly by the Gospel. Popular piety is a sign that the faith is spreading its roots into the heart of a people in such a way that it reaches into daily life. Popular religiosity is the first and fundamental mode of "inculturation" of the faith. While it must always take its lead and direction from the liturgy, it in turn enriches the faith by involving the heart.

We have thus moved from the somewhat negative clarifications, initially needed, to a positive definition of private revelations. How can they be classified correctly in relation to Scripture? To which theological category do they belong? The oldest letter of Saint Paul which has been preserved, perhaps the oldest of the New Testament texts, the First Letter to the Thessalonians, seems to me to point the way. The Apostle says: "Do not quench the Spirit, do not despise prophesying, but test everything, holding fast to what is good" (5:19-21). In every age the Church has received the charism of prophecy, which must be scrutinized but not scorned. On this point, it should be kept in mind that prophecy in the biblical sense does not mean to predict the future but to explain the will of God for the present, and therefore show the right path to take for the future. A person who foretells what is going to happen responds to the curiosity of the mind, which wants to draw back the veil on the future. The prophet speaks to the blindness of will and of reason, and declares the will of God as an indication and demand for the present time. In this case, prediction of the future is of secondary importance. What is essential is the actualization of the definitive Revelation, which concerns me at the deepest level. The prophetic word is a warning or a consolation, or both together. In this sense there is a link between the charism of prophecy and the category of "the signs of the times", which Vatican II brought to light anew: "You know how to interpret the appearance of earth and sky; why then do you not know how to interpret the present time?" (Lk 12:56). In this saying of Jesus, the "signs of the times" must be understood as the path he was taking, indeed it must be understood as Jesus himself. To interpret the signs of the times in the light of faith means to recognize the presence of Christ in every age. In the private revelations approved by the Church—and therefore also in Fatima—this is the point: they help us to understand the signs of the times and to respond to them rightly in faith.

THE ANTHROPOLOGICAL STRUCTURE OF PRIVATE REVELATIONS

In these reflections we have sought so far to identify the theological status of private revelations. Before undertaking an interpretation of the message of Fatima, we must still attempt briefly to offer some clarification of their anthropological (psychological) character. In this field, theological anthropology distinguishes three forms of perception or "vision": vision with the senses, and hence exterior bodily perception, interior perception, and spiritual vision (visio sensibilis - imaginativa - intellectualis). It is clear that in the visions of Lourdes, Fatima and other places it is not a question of normal exterior perception of the senses: the images and forms which are seen are not located spatially, as is the case for example with a tree or a house. This is perfectly obvious, for instance, as regards the vision of hell (described in the first part of the Fatima "secret") or even the vision described in the third part of the "secret". But the same can be very easily shown with regard to other visions, especially since not everybody present saw them, but only the "visionaries". It is also clear that it is not a matter of a "vision" in the mind, without images, as occurs at the higher levels of mysticism. Therefore we are dealing with the middle category, interior perception. For the visionary, this perception certainly has the force of a presence, equivalent for that person to an external manifestation to the senses.

Interior vision does not mean fantasy, which would be no more than an expression of the subjective imagination. It means rather that the soul is touched by something real, even if beyond the senses. It is rendered capable of seeing that which is beyond the senses, that which cannot be seen—seeing by means of the "interior senses". It involves true "objects", which touch the soul, even if these "objects" do not belong to our habitual sensory world. This is why there is a need for an interior vigilance of the heart, which is usually precluded by the intense pressure of external reality and of the images and thoughts which fill the soul. The person is led beyond pure exteriority and is touched by deeper dimensions of reality, which become visible to him. Perhaps this explains why children tend to be the ones to receive these apparitions: their souls are as yet little disturbed, their interior powers of perception are still not impaired. "On the lips of children and of babes you have found praise", replies Jesus with a phrase of Psalm 8 (v. 3) to the criticism of the High Priests and elders, who had judged the children's cries of "hosanna" inappropriate (cf. Mt 21:16).

"Interior vision" is not fantasy but, as we have said, a true and valid means of verification. But it also has its limitations. Even in exterior vision the subjective element is always present. We do not see the pure object, but it comes to us through the filter of our senses, which carry out a work of translation. This is still more evident in the case of interior vision, especially when it involves realities which in themselves transcend our horizon. The subject, the visionary, is still more powerfully involved. He sees insofar as he is able, in the modes of representation and consciousness available to him. In the case of interior vision, the process of translation is even more extensive than in exterior vision, for the subject shares in an essential way in the formation of the image of what appears. He can arrive at the image only within the bounds of his capacities and possibilities. Such visions therefore are never simple "photographs" of the other world, but are influenced by the potentialities and limitations of the perceiving subject.

This can be demonstrated in all the great visions of the saints; and naturally it is also true of the visions of the children at Fatima. The images described by them are by no means a simple expression of their fantasy, but the result of a real perception of a higher and interior origin. But neither should they be thought of as if for a moment the veil of the other world were drawn back, with heaven appearing in its pure essence, as one day we hope to see it in our definitive union with God. Rather the images are, in a manner of speaking, a synthesis of the impulse coming from on high and the capacity to receive this impulse in the visionaries, that is, the children. For this reason, the figurative language of the visions is symbolic. In this regard, Cardinal Sodano stated: "[they] do not describe photographically the details of future events, but synthesize and compress against a single background facts which extend through time in an unspecified succession and duration". This compression of time and place in a single image is typical of such visions, which for the most part can be deciphered only in retrospect. Not every element of the vision has to have a specific historical sense. It is the vision as a whole that matters, and the details must be understood on the basis of the images taken in their entirety. The central element of the image is revealed where it coincides with what is the focal point of Christian "prophecy" itself: the centre is found where the vision becomes a summons and a guide to the will of God.

AN ATTEMPT TO INTERPRET THE 'SECRET' OF FATIMA

The first and second parts of the "secret" of Fatima have already been so amply discussed in the relative literature that there is no need to deal with them again here. I would just like to recall briefly the most significant point. For one terrible moment, the children were given a vision of hell. They saw the fall of "the souls of poor sinners". And now they are told why they have been exposed to this moment: "in order to save souls"—to show the way to salvation. The words of the First Letter of Peter come to mind: "As the outcome of your faith you obtain the salvation of your souls" (1:9). To reach this goal, the way indicated — surprisingly for people from the Anglo-Saxon and German cultural world—is devotion to the Immaculate Heart of Mary. A brief comment may suffice to explain this. In biblical language, the "heart" indicates the centre of human life, the point where reason, will, temperament and sensitivity converge, where the person finds his unity and his interior orientation. According to Matthew 5:8, the "immaculate heart" is a heart which, with God's grace, has come to perfect interior unity and therefore "sees God". To be "devoted" to the Immaculate Heart of Mary means therefore to embrace this attitude of heart, which makes the fiat—"your will be done"—the defining centre of one's whole life. It might be objected that we should not place a human being between ourselves and Christ. But then we remember that Paul did not hesitate to say to his communities: "imitate me" (1 Cor 4:16; Phil 3:17; 1 Th 1:6; 2 Th 3:7, 9). In the Apostle they could see concretely what it meant to follow Christ. But from whom might we better learn in every age than from the Mother of the Lord?

Thus we come finally to the third part of the "secret" of Fatima which for the first time is being published in its entirety. As is clear from the documentation presented here, the interpretation offered by Cardinal Sodano in his statement of 13 May was first put personally to Sister Lucia. Sister Lucia responded by pointing out that she had received the vision but not its interpretation. The interpretation, she said, belonged not to the visionary but to the Church. After reading the text, however, she said that this interpretation corresponded to what she had experienced and that on her part she thought the interpretation correct. In what follows, therefore, we can only attempt to provide a deeper foundation for this interpretation, on the basis of the criteria already considered.

"To save souls" has emerged as the key word of the first and second parts of the "secret", and the key word of this third part is the threefold cry: "Penance, Penance, Penance!" The beginning of the Gospel comes to mind: "Repent and believe the Good News" (Mk 1:15). To understand the signs of the times means to accept the urgency of penance – of conversion – of faith. This is the correct response to this moment of history, characterized by the grave perils outlined in the images that follow. Allow me to add here a personal recollection: in a conversation with me Sister Lucia said that it appeared ever more clearly to her that the purpose of all the apparitions was to help people to grow more and more in faith, hope and love—everything else was intended to lead to this.

Let us now examine more closely the single images. The angel with the flaming sword on the left of the Mother of God recalls similar images in the Book of Revelation. This represents the threat of judgement which looms over the world. Today the prospect that the world might be reduced to ashes by a sea of fire no longer seems pure fantasy: man himself, with his inventions, has forged the flaming sword. The vision then shows the power which stands opposed to the force of destruction—the splendour of the Mother of God and, stemming from this in a certain way, the summons to penance. In this way, the importance of human freedom is underlined: the future is not in fact unchangeably set, and the image which the children saw is in no way a film preview of a future in which nothing can be changed. Indeed, the whole point of the vision is to bring freedom onto the scene and to steer freedom in a positive direction. The purpose of the vision is not to show a film of an irrevocably fixed future. Its meaning is exactly the opposite: it is meant to mobilize the forces of change in the right direction. Therefore we must totally discount fatalistic explanations of the "secret", such as, for example, the claim that the would-be assassin of 13 May 1981 was merely an instrument of the divine plan guided by Providence and could not therefore have acted freely, or other similar ideas in circulation. Rather, the vision speaks of dangers and how we might be saved from them.

The next phrases of the text show very clearly once again the symbolic character of the vision: God remains immeasurable, and is the light which surpasses every vision of ours. Human persons appear as in a mirror. We must always keep in mind the limits in the vision itself, which here are indicated visually. The future appears only "in a mirror dimly" (1 Cor 13:12). Let us now consider the individual images which follow in the text of the "secret". The place of the action is described in three symbols: a steep mountain, a great city reduced to ruins and finally a large rough-hewn cross. The mountain and city symbolize the arena of human history: history as an arduous ascent to the summit, history as the arena of human creativity and social harmony, but at the same time a place of destruction, where man actually destroys the fruits of his own work. The city can be the place of communion and progress, but also of danger and the most extreme menace. On the mountain stands the cross—the goal and guide of history. The cross transforms destruction into salvation; it stands as a sign of history's misery but also as a promise for history.

At this point human persons appear: the Bishop dressed in white ("we had the impression that it was the Holy Father"), other Bishops, priests, men and women Religious, and men and women of different ranks and social positions. The Pope seems to precede the others, trembling and suffering because of all the horrors around him. Not only do the houses of the city lie half in ruins, but he makes his way among the corpses of the dead. The Church's path is thus described as a Via Crucis, as a journey through a time of violence, destruction and persecution. The history of an entire century can be seen represented in this image. Just as the places of the earth are synthetically described in the two images of the mountain and the city, and are directed towards the cross, so too time is presented in a compressed way. In the vision we can recognize the last century as a century of martyrs, a century of suffering and persecution for the Church, a century of World Wars and the many local wars which filled the last fifty years and have inflicted unprecedented forms of cruelty. In the "mirror" of this vision we see passing before us the witnesses of the faith decade by decade. Here it would be appropriate to mention a phrase from the letter which Sister Lucia wrote to the Holy Father on 12 May 1982: "The third part of the 'secret' refers to Our Lady's words: 'If not, [Russia] will spread her errors throughout the world, causing wars and persecutions of the Church. The good will be martyred; the Holy Father will have much to suffer; various nations will be annihilated'".

In the Via Crucis of an entire century, the figure of the Pope has a special role. In his arduous ascent of the mountain we can undoubtedly see a convergence of different Popes. Beginning from Pius X up to the present Pope, they all shared the sufferings of the century and strove to go forward through all the anguish along the path which leads to the Cross. In the vision, the Pope too is killed along with the martyrs. When, after the attempted assassination on 13 May 1981, the Holy Father had the text of the third part of the "secret" brought to him, was it not inevitable that he should see in it his own fate? He had been very close to death, and he himself explained his survival in the following words: "... it was a mother's hand that guided the bullet's path and in his throes the Pope halted at the threshold of death" (13 May 1994). That here "a mother's hand" had deflected the fateful bullet only shows once more that there is no immutable destiny, that faith and prayer are forces which can influence history and that in the end prayer is more powerful than bullets and faith more powerful than armies.

The concluding part of the "secret" uses images which Lucia may have seen in devotional books and which draw their inspiration from long-standing intuitions of faith. It is a consoling vision, which seeks to open a history of blood and tears to the healing power of God. Beneath the arms of the cross angels gather up the blood of the martyrs, and with it they give life to the souls making their way to God. Here, the blood of Christ and the blood of the martyrs are considered as one: the blood of the martyrs runs down from the arms of the cross. The martyrs die in communion with the Passion of Christ, and their death becomes one

with his. For the sake of the body of Christ, they complete what is still lacking in his afflictions (cf. Col 1:24). Their life has
itself become a Eucharist, part of the mystery of the grain of wheat which in dying yields abundant fruit. The blood of the martyrs is the seed of Christians, said Tertullian. As from Christ's death, from his wounded side, the Church was born, so the death of the witnesses is fruitful for the future life of the Church. Therefore, the vision of the third part of the "secret", so distressing at first, concludes with an image of hope: no suffering is in vain, and it is a suffering Church, a Church of martyrs, which becomes a sign-post for man in his search for God. The loving arms of God welcome not only those who suffer like Lazarus, who found great solace there and mysteriously represents Christ, who wished to become for us the poor Lazarus. There is something more: from the suffering of the witnesses there comes a purifying and renewing power, because their suffering is the actualization of the suffering of Christ himself and a communication in the here and now of its saving effect.

And so we come to the final question: What is the meaning of the "secret" of Fatima as a whole (in its three parts)? What does it say to us? First of all we must affirm with Cardinal Sodano: "... the events to which the third part of the 'secret' of Fatima refers now seem part of the past". Insofar as individual events are described, they belong to the past. Those who expected exciting apocalyptic revelations about the end of the world or the future course of history are bound to be disappointed. Fatima does not satisfy our curiosity in this way, just as Christian faith in general cannot be reduced to an object of mere curiosity. What remains was already evident when we began our reflections on the text of the "secret": the exhortation to prayer as the path of "salvation for souls" and, likewise, the summons to penance and conversion.

I would like finally to mention another key expression of the "secret" which has become justly famous: "my Immaculate Heart will triumph". What does this mean? The Heart open to God, purified by contemplation of God, is stronger than guns and weapons of every kind. The fiat of Mary, the word of her heart, has changed the history of the world, because it brought the Saviour into the world—because, thanks to her Yes, God could become man in our world and remains so for all time. The Evil One has power in this world, as we see and experience continually; he has power because our freedom continually lets itself be led away from God. But since God himself took a human heart and has thus steered human freedom towards what is good, the freedom to choose evil no longer has the last word. From that time forth, the word that prevails is this: "In the world you will have tribulation, but take heart; I have overcome the world" (Jn 16:33). The message of Fatima invites us to trust in this promise.

Joseph Card. Ratzinger,
Prefect of the Congregation for the Doctrine of the Faith

(1) From the diary of John XXIII, 17 August 1959: "Audiences: Father Philippe, Commissary of the Holy Office, who brought me the letter containing the third part of the secrets of Fatima. I intend to read it with my Confessor".

(2) The Holy Father's comment at the General Audience of 14 October 1981 on "What happened in May: A Great Divine Trial" should be recalled: Insegnamenti di Giovanni Paolo II, IV, 2 (Vatican City, 1981), 409-412.

(3) Radio message during the Ceremony of Veneration, Thanksgiving and Entrustment to the Virgin Mary Theotokos in the Basilica of Saint Mary Major: Insegnamenti di Giovanni Paolo II, IV, 1 (Vatican City, 1981), 1246.

(4) On the Jubilee Day for Families, the Pope entrusted individuals and nations to Our Lady: Insegnamenti di Giovanni Paolo II, VII, 1 (Vatican City, 1984), 775-777.

(5) (Image) - not included here.

(6) In the "Fourth Memoir" of 8 December 1941 Sister Lucia writes: "I shall begin then my new task, and thus fulfil the commands received from Your Excellency as well as the desires of Dr Galamba. With the exception of that part of the Secret which I am not permitted to reveal at present, I shall say everything. I shall not knowingly omit anything, though I suppose I may forget just a few small details of minor importance".

(7) In the "Fourth Memoir" Sister Lucia adds: "In Portugal, the dogma of the faith will always be preserved, etc. ...".

(8) In the translation, the original text has been respected, even as regards the imprecise punctuation, which nevertheless does not impede an understanding of what the visionary wished to say.

The Message of Fatima

Pope John Paul II petitioning Our Lady of Fatima in Rome, 1984

Pope John Paul II with Sister Lucia, May 12, 2000 *Photo Purchased through AP WorldWide Photos*

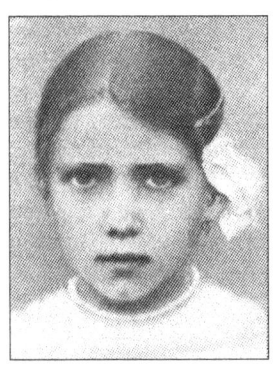

The Venerable
Jacinta Marto

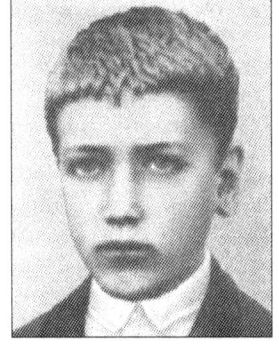

The Venerable
Francisco Marto

Sister Lucia today

**PHOTOCOPY OF THE HANDWRITTEN 'THIRD PART'
OF THE SECRET OF FATIMA**

CHAPTER SIX

ST. MICHAEL AND THE FLAMING SWORD OF FATIMA

It is with little fanfare that the account of the appearances of the angel at Fatima is noted in the history of the apparitions. Sister Lucia dos Santos, the lone surving visionary would later write in her memoirs that the angel looked so bright as to appear to be "wrapped in a sheet" and as white as "snow." This angel is believed by Church scholars who have studied and validated the events at Fatima in 1917 (The Catholic Church approved the apparitions of the Virgin Mary at Fatima on October 13, 1930.) to have been the legendary Archangel Michael, whose history is firmly recorded in the Old Testament and the New.

St. Michael the Archangel was revered as the guardian of Israel and the protector of synagogues and the Temple of Jerusalem. On the day of atonement, Jews concluded their prayers in a specific manner that invoked his intercession. "Michael, Prince of mercy, pray for Israel that it may reign in heaven." It is believed to have been Saint Michael who appeared to Abraham and forbade him to sacrifice his son Isaac. Likewise, according to Saint Gregory Nazianzen, St. Michael spoke to Moses and brought the plagues on Egypt. The great archangel is credited with leading the Israelites out of Egypt, across the Red Sea, and into the promised land and he fought with Lucifer (see the epistle of St. Jude 5-9) for the body of Moses. St. Michael led Joshua across the Jordan and delivered the three young men from the fiery furnace. He sent Habacuc to feed Daniel in the lion's den and when a war broke our with Persia, it was St. Michael who met with that nation's guardian angel.

The New Testament upholds his vital and significant role

throughout the unfolding of the Redemption, from beginning to end. Tradition holds that St. Michael announced to Saint Anne the Immaculate Conception of the Blessed Virgin Mary, freed St. Peter from prison, escorted the Virgin to Heaven during her Assumption and his legendary call in the final battle as announced in St. John's Apocalypse is well known. "Who is like unto God?"

That Fatima's story, as authoritatively documented and approved by the Catholic Church, begins with St. Michael is therefore not to be surprising for those who believe in what occurred there. For who other than Scripture's most celebrated defender of the faith could be expected to launch such a decisive fray. But with this understanding comes an equally important disclosure that may be surprising, for the story of Fatima does not begin in 1917 or 1915 for that matter, any more than the human events that led up to the great prophecies given there by the Virgin Mary in 1917. Rather, a series of events in Fatima some 800 years before is where our time frame for this story begins to unfold, and once again it is with St. Michael.

Accordingly, theologians and historians alike agree that a new era in human history started to dawn around the 12th century. Indeed, a profound and visible line of demarcation is noted during this period, as scholars note it seemed like the world suddenly moved in a way that was decidedly in favor of dispelling with matters of faith. For a while, things became so bad that even the Church seemed forced to contemplate the possibility of its extinction. Such was the rebellious nature of the times. Division was everywhere in the affairs of men and most visibly in the Church as a litany of controversial Popes came and went over the following centuries. Most significantly it was during the onset of this period of upheaval that we find a series of documented supernatural phenomen involving the Virgin Mary, St. Michael, the nation of Portugal and even the little village of Fatima.

In the year 1147, St. Michael reportedly appeared during the taking of the castle of Santarem from the Moors in Portugal by Alfonsus Henriques and the Christians. The victory was won on May 8th, 1147, (the anniversary of St. Michael's most famous apparition in a cave at Monte Gargano in Apulia, Italy, in the year 490) and laid the way for a series of reported supernatural events in Portugal. On the same day St. Michael appeared at Santarem, a second battle began in Lisbon that led to its liberation from the Moors on October 25, 1147. During this siege, a miracle of the sun is documented to have occurred. (This miracle is credited by the historian A. Fernando Castilho to have occurred on October 13th, the same date 770 years later that the great miracle of the sun occurred at the last apparition of the Virgin Mary at Fatima).

One hundred years later, in the year 1247, the second most famous Eucharistic miracle in Catholic Church history occurred at Santarem. More and more miracles continued to be reported during this period as a string of leaders in Portugal moved to firmly solidify the nation under the protection of St. Michael and the Blessed Virgin Mary.

Throughout the country, hundreds of churches were built and dedicated to the Virgin Mary or St. Michael, massive triumphal arches were erected, statues and images adorned the greatest buildings and at every funeral a banner of St. Michael was carried before the coffin to demonstrate his protection of souls. New monastaries, abbeys, and orders arose as Portugal, inside and out, firmly proclaimed itslef a nation consecrated to the faith.

In 1385, an army on the way to battle led by Nuno Alvares Pereira, later beatified by the Church, stopped in a church in a village named Ceica, in the country of Ouerem. (This would be in the diocese of Leira-Fatima today). Nuno reportedly asked for the intercession of the Virgin Mary to bring his army victory. The following day the army passed through what is today the village of Fatima. There, the entire army experienced a miracle in which the soldiers claimed to hear angels singing and to witness St. Michael raising his sword in a sign of victory. Nuno himself is then said to have rode through what became known as the Cova da Iria (the future meadow where the Virgin would appear in 1917). There, he was reportedly divinely told the ground he knelt on was holy and that one day God would bring victory over evil on this very spot and an era of peace would be granted to the world. (This miracle occurred on August 13th, 1385).

Nuno achieved his victory the next day, opening the way, even historians concur, for the great evangelization and exploration of the new world that would come from Portugal because of this significant event.

After this, more supernatural events are noted to have been reported in Portugal. Some fact, some legend, and many in the same diocese as the village of Fatima. Amongst the accounts were more reports of Marian apparitions which in retrospect perhaps signaled that the world was at a historical confluence. While not realized at the time, the medieval era was over and a new period, a renaissance age of esoteric ideas, laid summering beneath the surface, about to boil over in a volcanic eruption of unparralled social and cultural change. And for our purposes, a great battle between the spirits of light and the spirits of darkness had now begun.

EPILOGUE

"MEN MUST CEASE OFFENDING GOD"

Perhaps almost as surprising as Pope John Paul II's decision to announce the contents of the so called Third Secret of Fatima was the great length the Vatican went to prepare the manner in which the information would be released to the faithful. After first hearing through reliable sources that the Third Secret might be disclosed by the Pope during his May 13, 2000 visit to Fatima, the Vatican proceeded to not only announce the Secret's contents but went so far as to have the Prefect for the Congregation of the Doctrine of the Faith, Cardinal Joseph Ratzinger, issue a theological commentary on the meaning of the vision. This document, titled, *The Message of Fatima*, did more than just disclose the secret vision and the Cardinal's interpretation of its meaning. Rather, it elevated in a special way the significance of private revelations and how such events can have genuine importance to them.

While many more of the Church's feast days during the year stem from events related to private revelations than the average Catholic realizes, there has been a consistent effort by many in the Church over the centuries to downplay and trivialize the importance of reported apparitions, visions and other miraculous events. Now, with the release of Ratzinger's theological commentary on Fatima, the entire field of mystical theology has a new and relevant apologetic source. Indeed, the Cardinal's report is sure to be a reference paper in the future for the many issues that often surround private revelation in today's Church. In fact, I believe the historical significance of the document itself may some day eclipse the importance of its contents. This is because the

Church, in issuing such a document, explained to the faithful how a divine intervention by God can impact the present and the future mission of the Church in its march through history. Thus, Fatima is now doing what the Catechism of the Catholic Church states about private revelation. It is allowing the faithful to live more fully the will of God for the present, and as Ratzinger stated, to show us the right path to take for the future.

Of course, that path, the path to the Church's future, is especially noted in the contents of the *Message of Fatima*, for Mary's words at Fatima announced a coming "triumph" for the Church and an "era of peace" for mankind. But exactly when and how the fulfillment of this prophecy will take place in human events still remains a burning question for many devotees of Our Lady of Fatima. Ratzinger's attempt to interpret the Secret is helpful, but it was, as he himself noted, only an attempt; one limited by the mystery of understanding symbolic images that synthesize and compress facts that extend through time in an unspecified succession and duration.

However, Cardinal Ratzinger's report does help to show us where the world is today in the unfolding of the signs of our times. His assertion that "the vision of Fatima above all concerns the war waged by atheistic systems against the Church and Christians and the immense suffering endured by many because of this war" reveals that he sees an eschatological element associated with Fatima that is for the Church quite real and meaningful. This is confirmed by the words of Our Holy Father, Pope John Paul II: "Fatima is one of the greatest signs of the times in the 20th century because it announces many of the later events and conditions them on the response to its appeals." (October 24, 1997 L'Observatore Romano)

In contemplating all of this, I personally have come to believe that the contemporary revelations of the Virgin Mary should be used to help expand our understanding of what Cardinal Ratzinger meant in speaking of the atheistic powers that, in fact, still wage war against the Church. Mary's contemporary revelations tell us how such forces of evil have now progressed beyond the parameters of state militaristic designs of conquest and into the realm of philosophies and ideologies that infiltrate and destroy lives and souls through a society's culture. Subtly, for all intents and purposes, a "practical atheism" (as Mary calls it) has come to reign and rule in the hearts of many, especially in the west, which escaped the bondage of Communism. In so many words, the enemy is ourselves, not just atheistic regimens behind the former Iron Curtain and elsewhere, and peace is being threatened in ways that we don't understand – such as with the world wide epidemic of abortion, which, even more than the wars of the twentieth century, has caused the deaths of hundreds of millions. Indeed, these are the signs of the times . And truly, as long as the war on the unborn continues, Fatima will remain unfulfilled. Likewise, since Mary appeared at a place of such significance to the Moslem people (Fatima is the name of the daughter of Mohammed), there appears to be some role that the Moslem people must play in the coming fulfillment of Fatima's remaining prophecies.

But for the moment, mankind is in unchartered waters, hurling down a raging river that promises to bring us into a time and place in history that the world has never before seen. From the words of the three little prophets of Fatima over eighty years ago to the many prophetic voices of today, our planet is foretold to be scheduled for a date with destiny, a destiny that will bring great change into the world in order to fulfill Mary's promise at Fatima of an era of peace.

Will this peace come gently into the world or will the Angel with the flaming sword forge the way? The answer can perhaps be found in Our Lady's words at Fatima in 1917, "Men must cease offending God, Who is already so much offended."

> *"Throughout every century, in every land, there are stories of Mary coming from heaven to the aid of her children, often at the most desperate of times and in the most critical situations."*

APPENDIX ONE

A CLOSER LOOK AT THE VISION OF HELL CONTAINED IN THE FIRST PART OF THE SECRET OF FATIMA

From the Virgin Mary's apparitions at Fatima in 1917 has come the century's most powerful private revelation. On July 13th, the Virgin Mary appeared to three shepherd children at Fatima's Cova da Iria (Hollow of Irene) for the third time. In answer to the oldest visionary, Lucia dos Santó, the Virgin Mary promised that in October she would work a great miracle, "so that all might believe." After revealing this, Mary told the children to sacrifice themselves for sinners and to say, many times, a prayer she taught them.

Then, while speaking, the Virgin held out her hands, from which emanated bright rays that appeared to penetrate the earth. Suddenly, the ground vanished and the children found themselves standing on the edge of a sea of fire. As they stared into the vast lake of molten liquid, they saw a great number of devils and damned souls. The demons resembled black animals, each filling the air with shrieks, screams, and moaning cries. The souls, Lucia would later write, appeared to be in their bodies, rolling and trembling helplessly in the flames. They had no peace, even for a moment, and were constantly in pain, said Lucia. "You have seen Hell," Mary then told the children, "where the souls of sinners go."

Sister Lucia, in several of her Memoirs, detailed this horrifying vision. In the *First Memoir* (1935), she provided the following description:

That day, when we reached the pasture, Jacinta sat thoughtfully on a rock.

"Jacinta, come and play."

"I don't want to play today."

"Why not?"

"Because I'm thinking. The Lady told us to say the Rosary and to make sacrifices for the conversion of sinners. So from now on, when we say the Rosary we must say the whole Hail Mary and the whole Our Father! And the sacrifices, how are we going to make them?"

"Right away, Francisco thought of a good sacrifice: "Let's give our lunch to the sheep, and make the sacrifice of doing without it."

"In a couple of minutes, the contents of our lunch bag had been divided among the sheep. So that day, we fasted as strictly as the most austere Carthusian! Jacinta remained sitting on her rock, looking very thoughtful, and asked: "The Lady also said that many souls go to hell! What is hell, then?"

"It's like a big deep pit of wild beasts, with an enormous fire in it—that's how my mother used to explain it to me—and that's where people go who commit sins and don't confess them. They stay there and burn forever!"

"And they never get out of there again?"

"No!"

"Not even after many, many years?"

"No! Hell never ends!"

"And heaven never ends either?"

"Whoever goes to heaven, never leaves it again!"

"And whoever goes to hell, never leaves it either?"

"They're eternal, don't you see! They never end."

"That was how, for the first time, we made a meditation on hell and eternity. What made the biggest impression on Jacinta was the idea of eternity. Even in the middle of a game, she would stop and ask: "But listen! Doesn't hell end after many, many years then?"

"Or again: "Those people burning in hell, don't they ever die? And don't they turn into ashes? And if people pray very much for sinners, won't Our Lord get them out of there? And if they make sacrifices as well? Poor sinners! We have to pray and make many sacrifices for them!"

"Then she went on: "How good the Lady is! She has already promised to take us to heaven!"

In her *Third Memoir* (1941), Sr. Lucia provided an even more profound account of the vision of Hell:

"Well, the secret is made up of three distinct parts, two of which I am going to reveal. The first part is the vision of hell. Our Lady showed us a great sea of fire which seemed to be under the earth. Plunged in this fire were demons and souls in human form, like transparent burning embers, all blackened or burnished bronze, floating about in the conflagration, now raised into the air by the flames that issued from within themselves together with great clouds of smoke, now falling back on every side like sparks in a huge fire, without weight or equilibrium, and amid shrieks and groans of pain and despair, which horrified us and made us tremble with fear. The demons could be distinguished by their terrifying and repellent likeness to frightful and unknown animals, all black and transparent. This vision lasted but an instant. How can we ever be grateful enough to our kind heavenly Mother, who had already prepared us by promising in the first apparition, to take us to heaven. Otherwise, I think we would have died of fear and terror.

"We then looked up at Our Lady, who said to us so kindly and so sadly: "You have seen hell where the souls of poor sinners go. To save them, God wishes to establish in the world devotion to my Immaculate Heart. If what I say to you is done, many souls will be saved and there will be peace. The war is going to end: but if people do not cease offending God, a worse one will break out during the pontificate of Pius XI. When you see a night illumined by an unknown light, know that this is the great sign given you by God that He is about to punish the world for its crimes, by means of war, famine, and persecutions of the Church and of the Holy Father.

"To prevent this, I shall come to ask for the consecration of Russia to my Immaculate Heart, and the Communion of reparation on the First Saturdays. If my requests are heeded. Russia will be converted, and there will be peace: if not, she will spread her errors throughout the world, causing wars and persecutions of the Church. The good will be martyred; the Holy Father will have much to suffer; various nations will be annihilated. In the end, my Immaculate Heart will triumph. The Holy Father will consecrate Russia to me, and she will be converted, and a period of peace will be granted to the world."

In Sr. Lucia's *Fourth Memoir* (1941), she elaborated further on the vision of Hell with regard to Francisco Marto's vision of the devil:

"How different is the incident that I now call to mind. One day we went to a place called Pedreira, and while the sheep were browsing, we jumped from rock to rock, making our voices echo down in the deep ravines. Francisco withdrew, as was his wont, to a hollow among the rocks.

"A considerable time had elapsed, when we heard him shouting and crying out to us and to Our Lady. Distressed lest something might have happened to him, we ran in search of him, calling out his name.

"Where are you?"

"Here! Here!"

But it still took us some time before we could locate him. At last, we came upon him, trembling with fright, still on his knees, and so upset that he was unable to rise to his feet.

"What's wrong? What happened to you?"

"In a voice half smothered with fright, he replied: "It was one of those huge beasts that we saw in hell. He was right here breathing out flames!"

"I saw nothing, neither did Jacinta, so I laughed and said to him: "You never want to think about hell, so as not to be afraid; and now you're the first one to be frightened!"

"Indeed, whenever Jacinta appeared particularly moved by the remembrance of hell, he used to say to her: "Don't think so much about hell! Think about Our Lord and Our Lady instead. I don't think about hell, so as not to be afraid."

"He was anything but fearful. He'd go anywhere in the dark alone at night without the lightest hesitation. He played with lizards, and when he came across any snakes, he got them to entwine themselves round a stick, and even poured sheep's milk into the holes in the rocks for them to drink. He went hunting for foxes' holes and rabbits' burrows, and other creatures of the wilds."

Fatima writers have often alluded to how strongly affected Jacinta was by her experience of Hell. Indeed, although only a child, her great spirituality has often been attributed to the effects of the vision. Sr. Lucia commented on these effects in her *Third Memoir*:

"Your Excellency, as I already told you in the notes I sent to you after reading the book about Jacinta, some of the things revealed in the secret made a very strong impression on her. This was indeed the case.

The vision of hell filled her with horror to such a degree, that every penance and modification was as nothing in her eyes, if it could only prevent souls from going there.

"Well, I am going to answer the second question, one which has come to me from various quarters.

"How is it that Jacinta, small as she was, let herself be possessed by such a spirit of mortification and penance, and understood it so well?

"I think the reason is this: firstly, God willed to bestow on her a special grace, through the Immaculate Heart of Mary; and secondly, it was because she had looked upon hell, and had seen the ruin of souls who fall therein.

"Some people, even the most devout, refuse to speak to children about hell, in case it would frighten them. Yet God did not hesitate to show hell to three children, one of whom was only six years old, knowing well that they would be horrified to the point of, I would almost dare to say, withering away from fear.

"Jacinta often sat thoughtfully on the ground or on a rock, and exclaimed:

"Oh, Hell! Hell! How sorry I am for the souls who go to hell! And the people down there, burning alive, like wood in the fire!" Then, shuddering, she knelt down with her hands joined, and recited the prayer that Our Lady had taught us:

"O my Jesus! Forgive us, save us from the fire of hell. Lead all souls to heaven, especially those who are most in need."

Now Your Excellency will understand how my own impression was that the final words of this prayer refer to souls in greatest danger of damnation, or those who are nearest to it. Jacinta remained on her knees like this for long periods of time, saying the same prayer over and over again. From time to time, like someone awaking from sleep, she called out to her brother or myself:

"Francisco! Francisco! Are you praying with me? We must pray very much, to save souls from hell! So many go there! So many!" At other times, she asked: "Why doesn't Our Lady show hell to sinners? If they saw it, they would not sin, so as to avoid going there! You must tell Our Lady to show hell to all the people (referring to those who were in the Cova da Iria at the time of the Apparition). You'll see how they will be converted."

"Afterwards, unsatisfied, she asked me: "Why didn't you tell Our

Lady to show hell to those people?"

"I forgot," I answered.

"I didn't remember either!" she said, looking very sad.

"Sometimes, she also asked: "What are the sins people commit, for which they go to hell?"

"I don't know! Perhaps the sin of not going to Mass on Sunday, of stealing, of saying ugly words, of cursing and of swearing."

"So for just one word, then, people can go to hell?"

"Well, it's a sin!"

"It wouldn't be hard for them to keep quiet, and to go to Mass! I'm so sorry for sinners! If only I could show them hell!"

Suddenly, she would seize hold of me and say:

"I'm going to heaven, but you are staying here. If Our Lady lets you, tell everybody what hell is like, so that they won't commit any more sins and not go to hell."

"At other times, after thinking for a while, she said: "So many people falling into hell! So many people in hell!"

"To quiet her, I said: "Don't be afraid! You're going to heaven."

"Yes, I am," she said serenely, "but I want all those people to go there, too!"

"When, in a spirit of mortification, she did not want to eat, I said to her:

"Listen, Jacinta! Come and eat now."

"No! I'm offering this sacrifice for sinners who eat too much."

When she was ill, and yet went to Mass on a week day, I urged her:

"Jacinta, don't come! You can't, you're not able. Besides, today is not a Sunday!"

"That doesn't matter! I'm going for sinners who don't go on Sunday."

If she happened to hear any of those expressions which some people make a show of uttering, she covered her face with her hands and said:

"Oh, my God, don't those people realize that they can go to hell for saying those things? My Jesus, forgive them and convert them. They certainly don't know that they are offending God by all this! What a pity, my Jesus! I'll pray for them." There and then, she repeated the prayer that Our Lady had taught us: "Oh, my Jesus, forgive us...."

APPENDIX TWO

PENANCE, MARTYRDOM AND THE THIRD PART OF THE SECRET OF FATIMA

Found near the end of the Third Secret of Fatima text is a sequence of events that depict the journey of the faithful up a steep mountain towards the ultimate goal of the Christian life — salvation through the Cross of Jesus Christ. Angels are seen sprinkling the blood of the martyrs down upon the souls as they make their way up towards God. This striking image may be interpreted as a sign of great hope for our times as well as what the Church deems 'an invitation to the call to martyrdom.'

Martyrdom is commonly understood to mean the giving of one's life for the faith. Martyrs are said to go directly to heaven. The Church regards the crown of martyrdom as the greatest gift of God that one may obtain.

Martyrdom can take on more than one form. Two of the more common types of martyrdom are 'red' martyrdom and 'dry' martyrdom.

'Red' martyrdom is understood to mean the offering of one's own body to God for the 'sake of the kingdom' through the shedding of one's own blood. God has chosen many saints to receive this supreme calling. It must be noted that openness to the grace of God and acceptance of His Will completely are two of the necessary elements of becoming a martyr.

The Saints Respond to the Call to Martyrdom

Shortly after the time of the Apostles, terrible Christian persecution occurred in the Roman Colosseum. During this time, Turtullian said, 'The blood of the martyrs is the seed of the Church.' Martyrs have since come forward in every generation.

Over the centuries many popular known saints were given the gift of martyrdom, while some were not. For example, St. Francis of Assisi in his zeal to give his life for Christ went to foreign lands in the hopes to evangelize non-Christian nations. Knowing that these religions would be hostile towards Christianity, St. Francis desired to become a martyr for God, but to his surprise and to the surprise of his followers, St. Francis' life was not taken. Nor was it ever as St. Francis died of natural causes. Martyrdom can thus be seen as a gift given only to those special souls whom God Himself chooses.

Martyrdom and the Body

The thought of handing one's own body over to the hands of death is a reality that Christ himself faced. As martyrs unite their sufferings to the sufferings of Christ, one fact remains true - physical death is only the beginning of eternity with God in Heaven.

The North American martyr Isaac Jogues responded to the threat of having his body burned at the stake by saying, 'You can have my body, but my soul you cannot touch as it belongs to God.'

The Martyrs of the Twentieth Century

Two of the most important martyrs of the twentieth century are St. Maria Goretti and St. Maximillian Kolbe.

St. Maria Goretti was only twelve years old when her life was taken by a teenage boy who tried to rape her. Maria resisted him saying, 'No! No! No! What are you doing? Do not touch me! It is a Sin - You will go to Hell!" The boy would later convert from his ways and be forgiven by Assunta, St. Maria's mother. Both were present at her canonization in 1950.

Perhaps the most significant martyr of our times is St. Maximillian Kolbe. At the young age of 10 the Blessed Mother appeared to him holding in her hands both a red and a white crown. "Which of these crowns do you want Maximillian?' Mary asked. 'I'll take them both!' responded Kolbe eagerly. St. Maximillian would later wear the white crown of purity as a celibate in his priestly vocation and the red crown of martyrdom, giving his life at a concentration camp in Auschwitz. Kolbe truly lived the words of the Gospel, 'No greater love has this, than to lay down one's life for one's friend.'

Dry Martyrdom

Whether or not we are called to lay down our life for the 'Kingdom of Heaven' we are all called to a life of daily sacrifice and self-denial, also known as penance. This 'dry' martyrdom is referred to in Scripture, 'for whoever wishes to do my will, he must deny himself, take up his cross and follow after me.'

A lifetime of daily sacrifice and self-denial can be just as meritorious in the Lord's eyes as those who gave their bodies in becoming martyrs. A great example of this in our times is Mother Teresa. Her life's mission was spent serving the 'poorest of the poor.'

Pope John Paul II - Living Martyr?

Throughout Christian history, the call to martyrdom has had a powerful, transforming effect on the Church. Says Pope John Paul II, 'How many times, indeed, has the renewal of the Church been effected in blood?'

The call to martyrdom found in the Third Secret of Fatima is a sure sign that the Church will undergo trials and persecutions before a time of great renewal. Could this renewal be the 'Era of Peace' promised by Our Lady of Fatima in 1917?

Pope John Paul II's decision to release the Third Secret of Fatima further advances his fight against the culture of death. It is no surprise that he has been called Our Lady's Pope. He had been chosen to lead Mary's Triumph into the world. His depiction as a suffering servant of God in the Third Secret of Fatima vision further defines his role as a living martyr in the Church today.

(This chapter was written by Michael Fontecchio and originally appeared as an article in the Spring, 2001, Queen of Peace Newspaper - Secret of Fatima Edition.)

**Pope John Paul II
Praying the Rosary**

APPENDIX THREE

THE MIRACLE OF THE SUN AND THE SECRET OF FATIMA

Fatima was and remains a great message of light and hope for the world. It is a message of peace, prayer, and intercession. At Fatima, the Holy Spirit poured out His graces abundantly and any anxiousness arisen from Fatima's message is due to those who have not taken to heart Fatima's call to conversion. We especially find this with those who still express concern that Russia has not been consecrated in the prescribed manner. There is also concern for the many sensational writings associated with Fatima from other private revelations. Like the pseudo versions of the Third Secret, these writings are often filled with mystifications, caricatures, exaggerations, and sensationalism, contributing to an eschatology of calamity. The true and profound message of Fatima points to one thing: God's Love for His people and His desire that their happiness in this world and salvation in the next be obtained.

All of this constitutes the true message of Fatima as it does for all authentic apparitions and revelations. However, the message of Fatima does contain "certain highly dramatic aspects," notes Fr. Joacquin Maria Alonso, C.M.F., the internationally known theologian and expert on Fatima who was appointed by the Bishop of Leiria to prepare the definitive study of Fatima and its message. And it is these aspects that demand attention. "These dramatic aspects were in no way meant to fill us with fear," Fr. Alonso asserted in his writings, but he too noted that they were "deeply serious."

Indeed, the seriousness of Fatima in word and vision is inescapable to anyone who seriously studies its message. And if Fatima's message was serious decades ago, one certainly can see it must be even more serious today. In 1982, Pope John Paul II stated that the message of Fatima was "more urgent now than ever" and that the Church has a "duty" to be mindful of it. "The appeal of the Lady of the message of Fatima is so deeply rooted in the Gospel and the whole of Tradition that the Church feels that the message imposes a commitment upon her (May 13, 1982)."

Sr. Lucia concurs but has also said it is important for the world to respond. "The Blessed Virgin is very sad because no one heeds her message, neither the good nor the bad. The good continue in their life of virtue, but without paying attention to the message of Fatima. Sinners keep following the road of evil, because they fail to see the terrible chastisement that is about to befall them. Believe me, Father, God is going to punish the world and very soon." [Interview with Sister Lucia by Father Fuentes, December 26, 1957; published in The Secret of Fatima by Father Joacquin Alonso, Ravengate Press, Cambridge, 1990]. More recent interviews with Sister Lucia disclose her satisfaction that the consecration of 1984 saved the world from nuclear war. But she said that "the devil is rising... and working against God and His creation" (Christus magazine, Portugal, March 1998).

Sister Lucia's comments are significant because they address the importance of understanding the remaining prophecies of Fatima. It would be nice to simply extol the pius aspects of Fatima's message and refrain from the serious elements, but the lone surviving visionary of Fatima confronted the reality of the present situation decades ago: "No one heeds her (The Virgin Mary's) message good or bad. ... God is going to punish the world."

This reality, that our world is submerged in sin and not responding to Fatima's message, together with the understanding that two of Fatima's prophecies remain unfulfilled, both of which foretell a radical change for world, brings us to where we are today: at the doorstep of the fulfillment of Fatima's message, and therefore at the doorstep of the Triumph of the Immaculate Heart in the world. This conclusion is more than supposition. Mary has repeatedly stated in contemporary apparitions that her Triumph is imminent and even Pope John Paul II alluded to this in his book Crossing the Threshold of Hope: "...Mary appeared to the three children at Fatima in Portugal and spoke to them words that now, at the end of this century, seem close to their fulfillment."

Thus, in a way, we are back at Fatima on October 13, 1917, back to the moments when the great miracle unfolded that day. For it is in those moments that some Fatima experts believe we were symbolically shown what may lie ahead, what our future held, and how God was clearly inviting mankind to return to Him. John Haffert in his book Now, The Woman Shall

Conquer (1997), perhaps summarized this understanding best:

> In most of the books I have written I have stressed the importance of the miracle of Fatima. One cannot know the details well enough or review them too often. Even after I had talked to dozens of witnesses it was many years before I grasped the awesomeness of what happened and came to believe, with the celebrated Jesuit theologian and scientist, Fr. Pio Sciatizzi, S.J., that this was "the greatest most colossal miracle in history."
>
> "It had been raining heavily before the moment of the miracle. The great hollow of Fatima was a sea of water and mud. But immediately after the miracle (which lasted about 12 minutes) the sea of water and mud had vanished. It was like the miracle of the Red Sea.
>
> "The sun itself crashed down upon the earth. It was seen in a radius of 32 miles! It was like the miracle of the sun in the time of Joshua, when the fire of the sun appeared to act independently of the sun itself.
>
> "It was also like the miracle of Elias, who called fire from the sky so that all would believe that "God is God!...and the fire consumed, not only the sacrifice offered by the prophet, but the water in the trench around it.
>
> "Therefore this miracle of Fatima had the elements of the three greatest miracles of the Old Testament. What is more, NEVER BEFORE in history had God, "so that all may believe," performed a miracle at a PREDICTED TIME AND PLACE!
>
> "Perhaps the main reason why we feel compelled to look to Fatima as a mystical throne of the Queen of the World is because of the Miracle of the Sun. This unprecedented miracle recalls the description of Our Lady in the Apocalypse. Moreover, the essential power of the sun is atomic power, and the very "annihilation of nations" which Our Lady foretold in Her Fatima apparitions now threatens the world through nuclear weapons. Yet in demonstrating such power, in making such awesome prophecies at Fatima, our Queen could promise "an era of peace to mankind."

Indeed, the clear symbolism in the great miracle of the coming era of nuclear weapons and what this danger would mean to a world that further separated itself from God is well understood. It is the negative consequence of not returning to God, of not responding to Fatima's call. Quite simply, the world was being shown how the heavens could rain fire and destruction, a just punishment imposed upon ourselves. This understanding is reinforced in Lucia's memoirs when she states that of all Mary's words to her during the Fatima apparitions, the words said to her immediately before the great miracle of the sun were most memorable. These words can be understood to be of a "warning" nature and directly connected to the miracle that was about to occur just seconds later:

"Now Your Excellency, here we are at the 13th of October (1917).

You already know all that happened on that day. Of all the words spoken at this Apparition, the ones most deeply engraved upon my heart were those of the request made by our heavenly Mother:

"Do not offend Our Lord and God any more, because He is already so much offended!" How loving a complaint, how tender a request. Who will grant me to make it echo through the whole world, so that all the children of our Mother in heaven may hear the sound of her voice! Then, opening her hands, she made them reflect on the sun.

Lucia writes that the miracle of the sun then began to occur before the stunned onlookers. Researchers say it lasted about ten minutes. During the last phase many believed the sun would strike the earth and the end of the world would occur.

But if God presented in the miracle of the sun the negative consequences of mankind failing to respond to His call, could He perhaps have also symbolically revealed in this same miracle the positive consequences of mankind returning to Him, the deeper meaning of the peace He wished to give to the world.

Indeed, the fact that the sun halted its plunge and returned to its proper position in the sky has been understood to signal that in the end, even if mankind fails to choose to return to Him, God will not permit the evils of the world to bring it to "total" destruction. God will not permit Satan to triumph as Mary so clearly conveyed at Fatima. Therefore, if the terrible symbolism behind the falling sun at Fatima is not to be fulfilled in a negative consequence, then what else may have God been trying to tell us when He chose this miracle to fulfill the Virgin's promise of a "sign"? What other consequence could the falling sun perhaps represent in the great vision witnessed by tens of thousands on that day?

We can search through mountains of revelations since Fatima for greater insight but would probably be faced with attempting to construct a lengthy and hypothetical answer. It is no secret that Our Lady has alluded to intrinsic meanings of what the Triumph of the Immaculate Heart will bring. From crushing Satan's efforts to topple the Church to her direct role in saving mankind from nuclear annihilation, from unifying Christian denominations to bringing the world into a new era, Mary has indicated that the Triumph will mean many good things for the world, especially the Church. But one extraordinary and profound meaning stands out and needs to be pondered. It is one of a definitive nature and is most logical in lieu of Mary's efforts over the last two centuries. It is also an understanding that can be found symbolically in the falling sun, for it is one that is most fitting and appropriate to the reason behind the great miracle at Fatima. And that understanding is this: the miracle of the sun was actually a sign of the coming reunification of God the Father with His creation and with His children. It was a sign of a coming reunification with Him in spirit and in love, something that our Creator has desired for ages and is spoken of in Scripture. It was a sign of the coming of the restoration of God's Kingdom on earth as the Lord told the Apostles.

Indeed, the restoration of God the Father's Kingdom on earth "as it is in heaven" was at the center of Christ's message. Over and over Christ called our attention to the Father. Scripture prophetically speaks of the Father's Will to come on earth as it is in heaven (Mt 6:10), of the restoration of the Kingdom on earth at a time to be designated by the Father (Acts 1:6), and that the Father's Name, glorified by Christ during His Passion, is to be glorified again (Jn 12:28). A powerful reconnection in spirit with Our Father in heaven is, therefore, an undeniable part of the mission of the Church, although for the past 2,000 years this reunion has not been emphasized. In the past decade, Pope John Paul II has spoken of the "definitive coming of the Kingdom" and several prominent theologians, such as Rev. Bertrand de Margerie, Fr. Renee Laurentin, Fr. Michael O'Carroll, C.S.S.P. and Fr. Jean Galot, S.D., have studied this matter. If we look closely at their writings, we find more and more evidence that perhaps this time is near.

Fr. Jean Galot S.D. an eminent Biblical scholar and theologian, who teaches at the Pontifical Gregorian University in Rome and is the author of countless books and articles, addressed the issue in his book Abba Father: We Long to See Your Face (Alba House, New York, 1992). Fr. Galot went as far as to say that "the answer to all our problems is to be found in God the Father:

"Learning to know God our Father is the supreme achievement of theology and, in a more all-embracing way, of all human knowledge. Our intellects are made to know the truth, whose primordial origin is the Father. We can be fully satisfied in our intellectual search for God only when we draw from this primary source which is also the ultimate goal of all human knowledge.

"We must admit that until now scholarly effort to understand God our Father has not been as intense as it should have been. The most sublime object of all research and knowledge has not sufficiently challenged the minds of theologians. Our Christian faith has not adequately emphasized the person of God the Father, and liturgical worship has not focussed enough on this divine Person.

"Likewise, the kingdom whose coming is desired is the kingdom of the Father. It is, therefore, the reign of a fatherly love that gathers men into one sonship from which the closest brotherhood results. When Jesus said to "seek his kingdom," he was speaking to his disciples of the kingdom of "your Father" (cf. Lk 12:30-31). The fatherhood of God gives a new meaning to the kingdom.

"It this perspective, the words 'on earth as in heaven,' which apply to all three petitions, are given their full significance. The earth must become the image of heaven where there is perfect veneration of the name of the father, the absolute reign of his paternal love and the complete fulfillment of his fatherly will. Christians ask that the earthly world be increasingly modeled upon the heavenly realm. The mark of the "new-earth" is that it reflects heaven.

"It might surprise us that the building up of the new world is the object of petitions to the Father when it is the Father himself who has the supreme responsibility for his kingdom. Yet here we see a characteristic trait of paternal love. The Father wants his children to collaborate with him in every phase of his work. This collaboration takes the form of prayer first of all, prayer destined to have an impact on the development of the kingdom. The petitions are the means through which Christians can be assured of having a co-responsibility in the work of salvation, a co-responsibility exercised in a spirit of final dependence but guaranteed to have authentic efficacy. In this sense, the "Our Father" contributes to the enhancement of the human personality of its role in the universe."

APPENDIX FOUR

THE ROSARY AND THE SECRET OF FATIMA

On the wall of the Sistine Chapel, Michelangelo's *Last Judgment* is an awe-inspiring and intimidating painting of the power and glory of God. Completed in 1541 and recently refurbished, the painting projects the story of salvation like no other artwork.

Created during a time of crisis in the Church, the painting was a message from Michelangelo to the bishops and cardinals who met at the Council of Trent in 1545. This council's task it was to initiate the Counter-Reformation that would reaffirm the Church's doctrines and teachings. And in Michelangelo's work, they found the inspiration to do so.

The visual message of *The Last Judgment* preserved the Church doctrines on Mary, the Mother of God, and the honor accorded her. Michelangelo's great fresco let everyone see for themselves that Mary is forever at the side of her Son, reigning as Heaven's Queen and earth's model of discipleship. And Michelangelo's work was not lacking in depth of meaning, for he painted a huge *Rosary* that hung down over the ramparts of Heaven, a Rosary on which two souls grasp desperately as they pull their way into Paradise.

No word or image tells us better how important the Rosary is to the spiritual lives of the faithful, because for centuries Heaven has been calling souls to this mystery of salvation.

The prayer is said to have slowly evolved in Ireland and over the centuries developed in content and organization. Then, in 1214, the Virgin Mary reportedly appeared to St. Dominic and presented him with the Rosary as a powerful means of converting the Albigensian heretics and other sinners.

The Albigensian heresy rocked the 13th century Church in a frightful way. Tradition tells us that in a forest outside of Toulouse, Mary appeared to St. Dominic after he had been praying for three days and nights. Because of self-mortification, he had lapsed into a coma. At this point, the Virgin appeared and reportedly said, **"Dear Dominic, do you know which weapon the Blessed Trinity wants to use to reform the world?"**

"Oh, my Lady," replied St. Dominic, "you know far better than I do because next to your Son, Jesus Christ, you have always been the chief instrument of our salvation."

At this, Mary gave the Rosary to St. Dominic, explaining to him that it was **"the foundation stone of the New Testament."**

The saint returned to Toulouse, where he began to zealously preach the merits of the new prayer. Reportedly assisted by angels, he gave a sermon that was accompanied by the roar of heavenly thunder. The sky is said to have darkened, and the earth shook while flashes of lightning laced the heavens. Just as the crowd was overcome with fear, an image of Mary appeared. She raised her arms up and down to Heaven as if to call down God's wrath on the people if they did not convert. After this, townspeople repented and turned back to God, and devotion to the Rosary began to rapidly spread.

St. Dominic preached the spiritual benefits of Rosary for the rest of his life. However, within two centuries the prayer had almost disappeared as a devotion. In 1460, after receiving a special warning from the Lord, Blessed Alan de la Roche led a crusade to encourage use of the prayer.

Blessed Alan reportedly received a vision that showed how Jesus and Mary had appeared to St. Dominic to help him understand the power of the Rosary. He was told that Heaven wished this prayer to be firmly embraced by the faithful as the preferred weapon to combat evil.

Blessed Alan also received visions of Jesus and Mary and St. Dominic. Through his efforts, the Rosary was firmly reestablished throughout Europe. The faithful were taught how heaven wished souls to survive spiritually in a world besieged by Satan and his followers. Mary revealed that a spiritual war was unfolding, and the Rosary, with the Sacraments, was to be the ultimate weapon during this conflict.

After Blessed Alan restored the prayer in 1460, the Rosary became known as the Psalter of Jesus and Mary because it has the same number of Angelic Salutations as there are Psalms.

In his book, *The Secret of the Rosary*, St. Louis de Montfort explains why the Rosary is so powerful:

Since simple and uneducated people are not able to say the Psalms of David, the Rosary is held to be just as fruitful for them as David's Psalter is for others.

But the Rosary can be considered to be even more valuable than the latter for three reasons:

1. Firstly, because the Angelic Psalter bears a nobler fruit, that of the Word Incarnate, whereas David's Psalter only prophecies His (Christ's) coming.

2. Secondly, just as the real thing is more important than its prefiguration and as the body is more than its shadow, in the same way the Psalter of Our Lady is greater than David's Psalter which did no more than prefigure it;

3. And thirdly, because Our Lady's Psalter (or the Rosary made up of the Our Father and Hail Mary) is the direct work of the Most Blessed Trinity and was not made through a human instrument.

The Virgin Mary's Psalter is divided into three parts of five decades each for the following reasons:

1. To honor the three Persons of the Most Blessed Trinity
2. To honor the life, death, and glory of Jesus Christ
3. To imitate the Church Triumphant, to help the members of the Church Militant, and to lessen the pains of the Church Suffering
4. To imitate the three groups into which the Psalms are divided:
   a) The first being for the purgative life
   b) The second for the illuminative life
   c) The third for the unitive life
5. Finally, to give us graces in abundance during our lifetime, peace at death, and glory in eternity.

The word "Rosary" means "crown of roses," and thus, whenever a person devoutly prays the Rosary, wrote Blessed Alan de la Roche, he or she mystically places a crown of 153 red roses and 16 white roses on the heads of Jesus and Mary.

Blessed Alan taught these mysteries of the Rosary and its promises, and he also began to assemble an association, similar to an army, whose members would pledge to pray the Rosary and spread its devotion.

By the time Blessed Alan de la Roche died on Sept. 8, 1475, more than 100,000 people had joined the *Confraternity of the Rosary*, which he began.

Over the centuries, many great kings, popes, and saints courageously spread the Rosary, often crediting its miraculous power with securing Heaven's favors for both small and great successes.

St. Philip Neri, St. Bernard, St. Robert Bellarmine, St. Francis de Sales, St. Bonaventure, St. Gertrude, St. Ignatius Loyola, St. Teresa of Avila, and St. Louis de Montfort were all champions of the Rosary.

However, it was St. Louis de Montfort who specifically explained and promoted the Rosary's powers and its mysteries. These are the mysteries of Christ's life, death, and resurrection, mysteries that relate to His mother. Most importantly, St. Louis de Montfort tells us in *The Secret of the Rosary* why it is necessary to contemplate the mysteries of the Rosary in order to use the prayer to its fullest potential:

For, in reality, the Rosary said without meditating on the sacred mysteries of our salvation would be almost like a body without a soul: excellent matter but without the form, which is meditation, this latter being that which sets it apart from all other devotions.

The first part of the Rosary contains five mysteries: the first is the Annunciation of the Archangel St. Gabriel to Our Lady; the second, the Visitation of Our Lady to her cousin St. Elizabeth; the third, the Nativity of Jesus Christ; the fourth, the Presentation of the Child Jesus in the Temple and the Purification of Our Lady; and the fifth, the Finding of Jesus in the Temple among the doctors.

These are called the JOYFUL MYSTERIES because of the joy which they gave to the whole universe. Our Lady and the angels were overwhelmed with joy the moment when the Son of God was incarnate. St. Elizabeth and St. John the Baptist were filled with joy by the visit of Jesus and Mary. Heaven and earth rejoiced at the birth of Our Savior. Holy Simeon felt great consolation and was filled with joy when he took the Holy Child in his arms. The doctors were lost in admiration and wonderment at the answers which Jesus gave, and how could anyone describe the joy of Mary and Joseph when they found the Child Jesus after He has been lost for three days?

The second part of the Rosary is also composed of five mysteries which are called the SORROWFUL MYSTERIES because they show us Our Lord weighed down with sadness, covered with wounds, laden with insults, sufferings, and torments. The first of these mysteries is Jesus' Prayer and Agony in the Garden of Olives; the second, His scourging; the third, His Crowning with Thorns; the fourth, Jesus carrying His Cross; and the fifth, His Crucifixion and Death on Mount Calvary.

The third part of the Rosary contains five other mysteries, which are called the GLORIOUS MYSTERIES because when we say them, we meditate on Jesus and Mary in their triumph and glory. The first is the Resurrection of Jesus Christ; the second, His Ascension into Heaven; the third, the Descent of the Holy Ghost upon the Apostles; the fourth, Our Lady's glorious Assumption into Heaven; and the fifth, her Crowning in Heaven.

Thus, the prayer of the holy Rosary, together with meditation on its sacred mysteries, is a sacrifice of praise to God in thanksgiving for the great graces of our redemption. It is also, St. Louis de Montfort said, a holy reminder of the sufferings, death, and glory of Jesus Christ, all of which help perfect the spiritual maturity of a soul. Faithfully reciting the Rosary gives a soul the following graces:

1) a perfect knowledge of Jesus Christ
2) a purification of soul and a washing away of sin
3) victory over enemies
4) an increased ease in the practice of virtue
5) a love for Jesus Christ
6) an enrichment in graces and merits
7) the graces necessary to pay all our debts to God and our fellow men

Over the centuries, Mary revealed to visionaries, mystics, and saints how the Rosary melts the most hardened hearts of the greatest sinners. The Rosary creates a fervor for God in us, she said, and produces change in lives. Most of all, it appeases God's justice.

Indeed, it is this need the Virgin often invokes when imploring us to pray the Rosary. Mary pleads for faithful souls and nations to pray her Rosary to restrain the arm of her Son's coming justice.

While some dispute St. Dominic's role in originating the Rosary, five popes have credited him with founding it. Even though its full history remains a mystery, the accounts of its many successes are not.

Just 30 years after the Council of Trent's first session, a greatly outnumbered force of Christian defenders repelled a Turkish invasion on Oct. 7, 1571, off the coast of Greece at the Gulf of Lepanto. It was considered a miraculous victory brought about specifically by the Rosary, when St. Pius V led a Rosary Crusade that united all Europe in prayer. From this, the Feast of the Most Holy Rosary was established in 1573 and is still celebrated to this day on Oct. 7th.

Even before the battle of Lepanto, the Rosary was officially credited with bringing a miraculous victory in 1474 to the city of Cologne, which was under attack by Bergundian troops. After Lepanto, another victory over the Turks at Peterwardein in Hungary, by Prince Eugene on Aug. 5, 1716. The Feast of Our Lady of the Snows led Pope Clement XI to extend the Feast of the Most Holy Rosary to the Universal Church.

By the 19th century, so numerous were the miraculous favors credited to the Rosary, that popes began to recognize it as an institution in the Church. During his 25-year reign from 1878 to 1903, Pope Leo XIII wrote 12 encyclical or apostolic letters on the Rosary and its devotion. He attempted to use the Rosary to bring unity to the Church, and his writings "officially" credited the Rosary with the Church's victories of the past.

In *Supremi Apostolatus officio,* Pope Leo XIII began the recognition of October as the month of special devotion to the Rosary. In his letter *Salutaris ille,* published on Dec. 24, 1883, he called on each family to recite the Rosary daily, and in his letter of Sept. 20, 1887, he elevated the feast day to what it is today.

Most significantly, in his September 1892 encyclical, *Magnae Dei Matris,* he stressed the importance of the Rosary as the most appropriate form of prayer to Mary, saying that through the Rosary the great mysteries of our faith can be unlocked. In his 25-year reign, Pope Leo XIII touched on all aspects of the Rosary devotion, elevating it in a landmark way and setting the stage for the 20th century devotion to Mary.

In her last apparition at Fatima, on Oct. 13, 1917, the Virgin Mary told the children that she was "The Lady of the Rosary." Appearing with the Rosary in her right hand and the Brown Scapular in her left, she evoked the memory of what she told St. Dominic centuries before: **"one day the Rosary and the Scapular will save the world."**

According to visionaries and even several popes, that day is today.

Beginning with her apparitions at Rue de Bac, Paris, in 1830 until the modern era of Mary, the importance of the "Rosary Crusade" is indisputable.

From Lourdes in 1858, where the Virgin called for penance and the recitation of the Rosary, to Pontmain on Jan. 17, 1871, where the children reported that each time the people prayed the Rosary, the image of Mary in the sky increased in size, the Virgin has continuously invoked this devotion in her apparitions.

When at Fatima she foretold a dangerous future for the world, the Queen of the Most Holy Rosary made it clear this prayer would be the solution to the problems of a world headed into the nuclear age because a critical time in history was coming, a time when "annihilation" was only moments away. The faithful needed to be prepared for those decisive moments.

Pope Paul VI echoed this belief in his encyclical *Signum Magnum*, issued when he visited Fatima on May 13, 1967. And on May 13, 1971, the 25th anniversary of the proclamation of Pope Pius XII, pilgrim statues of Our Lady of Fatima were crowned throughout the world.

Today, Church leaders, and even Sr. Lucia, say it is evident that Our Lady is winning the war against Satan, and she is winning through the power of the Rosary. It is a power that will bring the final victory foretold at Fatima. Even *The Wall Street Journal* made this observation in a published report September 27th, one month after the failed coup in the Soviet Union that began on August 17, 1991. It quoted Pope John Paul II as stating, "the collapse of Communism ... compels us to think in a special way about Fatima."

Indeed, Mary's promise of a great victory for God through the Rosary is reaffirmed time and again through historical events. It was reportedly on Oct. 13, 1886, that Pope Leo XIII, the great champion of the Rosary, received his vision of the coming confrontation between Satan and God. And it was in October 1917 that St. Maximilian Kolbe founded the Militia Immaculata, one of the greatest movements ever "to win the world for Mary." The victory would be obtained, Kolbe told his followers, by "fingering the beads of the Rosary."

Once again, we must note that the Jesuit priests were praying the Rosary at Hiroshima on the fateful day of Aug. 6, 1945, when they were spared death from the atomic blast. (August 6th is also the date St. Dominic died [August 6, 1221]). The same thing occurred at Nagasaki, where the Fatima prayers reportedly preserved the lives of a group of friars who were at ground zero of the atomic blast and survived without any radiation effects. It was the Rosary that 70,000 people promised to pray in Austria for seven years before the Soviets departed on May 13, 1955. Furthermore, it was the Rosary that more than 600,000 women in Brazil joined together to pray to derail a communist takeover in Brazil in 1962.

A series of unexplainable events on Fatima anniversary dates involving the Soviet Union surrounds the Cold War era of 1960 through 1990 and must be noted in recognition of the power of the Rosary. Marian experts say.

On October 12-13, 1960 another major intercession by Mary is believed to have possibly prevented the world from experiencing nuclear destruction. Father Albert Shamon, in his book *The Power of the Rosary*, relays this amazing story:

Most of us remember the time when Nikita Khrushchev visited the United Nations in October, 1960 and boasted that "they would bury us"—would annihilate us! And to emphasize his boasting, he took off his shoe and pounded the desk before the horrified world assembly.

This was no idle boast. Khrushchev knew his scientists had been working on a nuclear missile and had completed their work and planned in November 1960, the 43rd anniversary of the Bolshevik Revolution, to present it to Khrushchev.

But here's what happened. Pope John XXIII had opened and read the Third Fatima Secret given to Sister Lucy. He authorized the Bishop of Leiria (Fatima) to write to all the bishops of the world, inviting them to join with the pilgrims of Fatima on the night of October 12-13, 1960, in prayer and penance for Russia's conversion and consequent world peace.

On the night of October 12-13, about a million pilgrims spent the night outdoors in the Cova da Iria at Fatima in prayer and penance before the Blessed Sacrament. They prayed and watched despite a penetrating rain which chilled them to the bone.

At the same time at least 300 dioceses throughout the world joined with them. Pope John XXIII sent a special blessing to all taking part in this unprecedented night of reparation.

On the night between October 12 and 13, right after his shoe-pounding episode, Khrushchev suddenly pulled up stakes and enplaned in all haste for Moscow, cancelling all subsequent engagements. Why?

Marshall Nedelin, the best minds in Russia on nuclear energy, and several government officials were present for the final testing of the missile that was going to be presented to Khrushchev. When countdown was completed, the missile, for some reason or other, did not leave the launch pad. After 15 or 20 minutes, Nedelin and all others came out of the shelter. When they did, the missile exploded killing over 300 people. This set back Russia's nuclear program for 20 years, prevented all-out atomic warfare, the burying of the U.S.-and this happened on the night when the whole Catholic world was on its knees before the Blessed Sacrament, gathered at the feet of our Rosary Queen in Fatima.

On May 13, 1984, as one of the greatest crowds ever to come to Fatima celebrated the anniversary of the Virgin's first apparition there by praying the Rosary, another significant event occurred that would again help "to prevent" nuclear conflict.

On that day, a massive explosion eliminated two-thirds of the surface to air and ship to ship missiles of the Soviet Union's most powerful fleet, the Northern Fleet.

According to *Jane's Defense Weekly* of London, this was "the greatest disaster to occur in the Soviet navy since WW II." Could this have been an accident of great significance? According to Sister Lucia of Fatima, "a nuclear war would have occurred in 1985." (Source: *The Triumphant Queen of the World,* 1995 by Daniel J. Lynch)

Four years later, another event happened. As thousands prayed all night long on May 12, 1988, during the vigil of the anniversary of the apparitions at Fatima, another major explosion shut down the Soviet Union's sole missile motor plant. The Associated Press reported at the time, "A major explosion has shut down the only plant in the Soviet Union that makes the main rocket motors of that country's newest long-range nuclear missile, according to U.S. officials." The Pentagon released a statement noting the accident occurred on May 12th and "destroyed several buildings at a Soviet propellant plant in Paulogriad."

Curiously, just a week before, on May 3, 1988, a similar eruption ripped apart a Nevada facility believed to be handling the ammonium perchlocate used in the main rocket motor for the SS-24.

Since 1989, many believe the power of the Rosary is slowly but surely bringing victory. The peaceful collapse of communism in Eastern Europe, the Soviet Union, Nicaragua, El Salvador, and other Soviet satellite countries is proof, along with the relatively peaceful overturning of dictatorships in countries like Panama, Grenada, and the Philippines.

In addition, the end of apartheid and the quick resolution of the Persian Gulf War should also be recognized as evidence, some say, of Mary's mighty intercession for her children through their prayers, especially the Rosary.

Now visionaries say Mary's triumph will come and it will occur through her intercession and the power of prayer. But many note that the Triumph of the Immaculate Heart has still not come, and therefore, many more Rosaries need to be prayed.

Indeed, a Rosary crusade is perhaps needed now more than ever. And because of the great danger of our times, it must be a crusade greater than ever before, for it will culminate in Mary's securing her final victory and preventing nuclear disaster.

"Say the Rosary every day," Mary told the three children at Fatima (at six of the apparitions in 1917), **"to obtain peace for the world."**

On December 10, 1925, and then again on June 13, 1929 Mary appeared to Sister Lucia in a convent in Tuy, Spain, to fulfill her promise of coming to ask for the consecration of Russia to her Immaculate heart and the Communion of Reparation on the five first Saturdays.

In a letter written by Sister Lucia in the 1930's, she makes it clear that reparation to the Immaculate Heart of Mary is necessary and that the practice of reparation is ultimately intended to bring about the true conversion of Russia through the collegial consecration.

Sister Lucia said the Virgin asks the following:

1) **PRAY THE ROSARY**
2) **WEAR THE SCAPULAR** (Mary appeared at Fatima on October 13th in one of the final visions to the children holding a Brown Scapular, the Scapular of Mt. Carmel, in her left hand. The Scapular is considered a sign of consecration to the Immaculate Heart of Mary.)
3) **MAKE THE COMMUNION OF REPARATION OF THE FIRST SATURDAY OF EACH MONTH. THIS INCLUDES CONFESSION, COMMUNION, ROSARY, AND SPEND AT LEAST 15 MINUTES IN MEDITATION UPON THE MYSTERIES OF THE ROSARY.**

In an historic interview on Oct. 11, 1993, Sister Lucia said:

> "All the wars which have occurred could have been avoided through prayer and sacrifice. This is why Our Lady asked for the Communion of Reparation and the Consecration. People expect things to happen immediately within their own time frame. But Fatima is still in its third day. The Triumph is an on going process. We are now in the post consecration period. Fatima has just begun. How can one expect it to be over immediately? The Rosary, which is the most important spiritual weapon in these times, when the devil is so active, is to be recited."

NOTES

CHAPTER ONE:
WHY DOES MARY APPEAR?
    The accounts of Saragozza and Le Put, France are from Michael Brown's book *The Last Secret* which I highly recommend. The following references are all excellent sources for information on documented reports of apparitions: *True and False Apparitions in the Church* by Bernard Billet, *Apparitions* by C.M. Staehlen, *Entu to Sur Les Apparitions de La Vierge* by Yves Chiron, *Religious Apparitions and The Cold War in Southern Europe* by William A. Christian Jr., *Lexicon der Marienerschermungen* by Robert Ernst, *Les Apparitions de La Virege* by Sylvie Barnay. Barnay's work and Chiron's study are part of the listed apparitions of Dayton University's Marian Research Institute's web page.
    The Day Will Come (1996) by Michael Brown, *A Guide to Apparitions of the Blessed Virgin Mary* (1995) by Peter Heinz, and *Erscheinungen und Borschaften der Gottesmutler Maria* (1995) are also excellent sources for apparitions. All three works are by lay people.
    The quotes by historian Thomas Kselman are from his book *Miracles and Prophecies In Nineteenth Century France,* pages 61 and 62. This book is highly recommended. The quote from Professor David Blackbourn is from his book, *Marpingen,* page 5. Marpingen is also highly recommended and is available at local bookstores.

CHAPTER TWO:
MARIAN SECRETS – A CONTROVERSIAL SUBJECT
    Sister Lucia's quote is from *Fatima, in Lucia's Own Words,* page 19. St. Catherine Laboure's quote is from the book *Saint Catherine Laboure of Sister Mary of the Holy Trinity* by Father Joseph Dirvin (Tan books).
Most of the account of the unfolding of the Secrets of La Salette comes from the book *Encountering Mary* by Sandra L. Zimdars-Swartz, pages 165-189. This book is highly recommended.

CHAPTER THREE:
NINETEENTH CENTURY VISIONS FORESHADOW FATIMA
    The information on Marie Julie Jahenny's life and revelations comes from *The Prophecies of La Fraudais* by Pierre Roberdel.
    Many of the 19th century prophets, prophecies and apparitions cited in

this chapter are from Thomas Kselman's book *Miracles and Prophecies in Nineteenth Century France*, David Blackbourn's *Marpingen*, , and *Lexicon der Marienerschermungen* by Robert Ernst. Michael Browns, *The Last Secret* was also referenced. However a significant number of apparitions were singled out from dozens of books either read or researched over many years. I have listed them in the bibliography.

The secrets of La Salette comes from the booklet *Apparitions of the Virgin Mary on the Mountain of La Salette* published by the Shepherdess of La Salette and printed in America by the Gregorian Press in Berlin, N.J. The story of St. John Vianney is from Tan Books *Cure of Ars* by Father Bartholomew O'Brien. The message of our Lady of Akita is from *Akita, The Tears and Messages* by Teiji Yasuda, O.S.V.. Blackbourn's account of Elisa Rectenwald is from his book, *Marpingen*, page 326. Kselman's observation is from his book *Miracles and Prophecies in Nineteenth Century France*, page 122. William A. Christian's quote is from his book *Visionaries, The Spanish Republic and the Reign of Christ*, pages 2 and 3.

The 19th century military facts comes from Hugh Thomas's *A History of the World*.

CHAPTER FOUR:
THE FATIMA PROPHECIES

Many of the 19th century prophets, prophecies and apparitions cited in his chapter are from Thomas Kselman's book *Miracles and Prophecies in Nineteenth Century France*, David Blackbourn's *Marpingen*, , and *Lexicon der Marienerschermungen* by Robert Ernst. Michael Browns, *The Last Secret* was also referenced. However a significant number of apparitions were singled out from dozens of books either read or researched over many years. I have listed them in the bibliography.

Padre Pio's quotes are from *Padre Pio:The True Story* by C. Bernard Ruffen, I also used *Padre Pio,The Stigmatist* by Rev. Charles Mortimar Carty. Mary's prophecies at Fatima are documented in almost every book writen about the apparitions at Fatima. Many such books are in the bibliography. Pope Benedict's XV's quotes is from an article by L. Edward Cole in *Soul Magazine*, Nov.–Dec 1990. The event os the Bolshevick Revolution were taken primarily from Hugh Thomas's *A History of the World*. Berthe Petit's quote is taken from my book *Call of the Ages*. The Theresa Neuman account is from *Theresa Neuman, Mystic and Stigmatist* by Adalbert Vogl. The Marthe Robin quote is from John Haffert's book *Her Words to the Nuclear Age*. William A. Christian's quote is from his book *Visionaries*, page XX. Sister Consolata Betrone's quote is from thee book *Jesus Appeals to the World* by Lorenzo Sales, I.M.C. (Abba House, New York). Sister Faustina Kowalska's message is from her diary, *Divine Mercy in My Soul*, page 322, (Stockbridge, Massachusetts, Marian Press 1987).

CHAPTER SIX:
ST. MICHAEL AND THE FLAMING SWORD OF FATIMA

The information on St. Michael and Fatima comes from the book, *St. Michael and the Fatima Connection,* by Carlos Evaristo (available at Fatima). The onset of the Renaissance and its philosophical and political ramifications are discussed in many history books. I used several, most notably *A History of the World* by Hugh Thomas.

THE 'THIRD SECRET OF FATIMA VISION' ARTWORK

"**N**ecessity" is indeed "the mother of invention." To me, this has always meant that God gives grace when it is needed, and not before. This was certainly the case while creating the artwork of the Third Secret of Fatima Vision. I will always be grateful to God for the light He shines just ahead of my footsteps.

As an illustrator, I often draw inspiration and information from written texts. Creating images that "tell the story" is really a form of translating ... words into pictures. The same concepts, thoughts, and ideas that gave birth to the text should be faithfully expressed in the finished artwork. With the Third Secret of Fatima Vision artwork, it became important not to say something that would be inconsistent with the actual "third secret" text or the various texts released by the Vatican. Fidelity to the truth is paramount.

The actual "third secret" text is fairly short and somewhat cryptic to modern ears. It describes a series of images as they move past a stationary viewer ... much like a person watching a movie trailer. Without an overview of the movie's plot, the meaning of the disjointed images can be unclear. My task was to make a single image that conveyed the essential elements and meanings of that "moving picture."

The input of the St. Andrew's Productions staff was invaluable in getting me started. Their imaginations had worked on the "third secret" text long enough to produce some good fruit. I wanted to pick it! Their comments helped me to establish some guidelines for the main elements; Our Blessed Mother, the Angel (to be depicted as St. Michael) and the "rough hewn cross." Central to their input was the necessity of keeping the overall tone hopeful and faithful to Rome. These two criteria became the umbrella under which I worked.

Common sense often plays an important role in representational art because it can connect the artist to the viewer with the power of a shared conviction. Certain basic visual elements of the "third secret" artwork simply had to "make sense." The appearance and interaction of the main characters had to be strong. The "third secret" text, however, was confusing regarding body positioning and gestures. It took several readings of the text, and numerous preliminary sketches, just to work out the staging of the Blessed Mother and the Angel so they were convincing, natural looking, and carrying out their missions as described in the text.

The Blessed Mother is depicted as a young woman, dressed in white as Our Lady of Fatima, standing in the familiar Our Lady of Grace pose. Her intervention in the actions of the Angel is carried out with the delicacy of a young maiden and the brilliance and strength of God's perfect instrument. Her gaze is maternal and is directed at the world and the souls below. She is a conduit of grace which comes from above and which flows from her outstretched hands.

The Angel is depicted as St. Michael. His open wings, flowing hair and cloak convey his agility as a messenger of God. His strong right arm symbolizes his will to accomplish God's errand. He points to his subject and we can follow the words of his message, "Penance, Penance, Penance" down to the world. He is armed with God's power, symbolized by the flaming sword in his left hand. He and the Blessed Mother are both sent by the same God. Their interaction is not in conflict, it is, instead, truly complimentary. Together they represent the entire truth being revealed ... the mystery of God's mercy and justice.

The upper two-thirds of the painting deals with God's messengers. The bottom third deals with the earthly elements. The text describes a procession of images that pass by the viewer ... the parade of man's history. The artwork picks up on the journey motif, starting in the distance at the far left, proceeding up a steep mountain, into and across the ruins of the central middle ground, and arriving at the summit on the right. The landscape is vast, steep, barren, desolate and finally fertile and green at the foot of the cross. The cross is unusual in its appearance. Its form is organic and dripping blood.

Traversing the landscape are people from various ranks and positions in life. Clearly represented are lay people, children, business people, women religious, priests, bishops (including members of the

Eastern Rite), cardinals and the white-robed figure of the Pope. There are also military figures in both threatening and non-threatening postures. The various figures are moving with determination along the journey toward the cross. There are however, casualties along the way. There is a fallen figure in the left foreground and the Pope and bishops are seen faltering. Angels are seen carrying out their respective missions, collecting the blood which drips from the cross (the blood of the martyrs mingled with the blood of Christ) and then sprinkling it with crystal aspersoriums in benediction on the travelers. The sojourners are not unaware of the drama that surrounds them. A woman religious pauses to pray for a fallen soul and a woman and child are seen, amidst the ruins, looking back over their shoulders at the sight. This cast of characters represents the Church Militant.

Many of the figures in the bottom third of the painting are not shown at the climax of the actions as described in the "third secret" text. They are, instead, shown in anticipation of the climax. This approach serves to maintain the element of hopefulness as well as to support an openness to interpretation. The artist and the staff of St. Andrew's Productions did not want to encourage alarmist conclusions to the Third Secret of Fatima Vision. Conclusions about the imminent nuclear chastisement of the world or the certainty of the assassination of a Pope are not supported by this artwork. What has been represented, however, is the reality of war, violence and destructive forces unleashed by man against man. This is an historical fact. The Holy Father is seen as fallen but not yet finished. His eventual death as a human being is not in question … its exact cause remains uncertain. What is certain is that he has suffered the pain caused by real bullets and the injuries caused by the arrows of criticism, lies and betrayal. What the vision and the artwork depict, not predict, is the triumph of the cross.

In conclusion, the Third Secret of Fatima Vision artwork is an attempt to translate the content and intent of the text into a single picture. The artwork was undertaken and completed with a desire to be faithful to the truth and the Church and to the grace given to meet the necessity of a production deadline. The painting has been reproduced in newspapers, framed and unframed prints, on the world wide web and on the cover of a book. My hope is that it helps convey the hopeful message of God's love for mankind and the wonderful reality of Our Blessed Mother's role in salvation history … and our history. I am grateful to the staff of St. Andrew's Productions for commissioning the artwork. I offer this account of my thoughts on the image for the good it may bring the viewers.

Thanks Mike!

Christopher J. Pelicano
Art Services
Easley, SC
September 10, 2001

Copyright © 2001 St. Andrew's Productions. All World Rights Reserved

THE 'THIRD SECRET OF FATIMA' VISION

Special Edition Prints Available!

Prayer Card	$ 1.00	*Includes Shipping*
8 x 10" Print Only	$ 5.00	+ $2.00 S/H
8 x 10" Gold Frame	$26.00	+ $6.00 S/H
12 x 16" Print Only	$ 8.00	+ $4.00 S/H
12 x 16" Gold Frame	$50.00	+ $10.00 S/H

20 x 24" Gicleé Gold Framed Print on 100% cotton paper, $200 + Call for Shipping/Insurance

**TO ORDER CALL: 1-412-787-9735
PLEASE CALL FOR QUANTITY PURCHASES**

Help Spread the *'Queen of Peace'* Newspaper!

1 copy - $3.00	**TO ORDER CALL - 412-787-9791**
25 copies - $20.00	
50 copies - $36.00	Order the *Queen of Peace* Newspapers in Quantity and Save!
100 copies - $60.00	Prices Include Shipping and Handling
Over 100 copies - Call	★ Newspaper Special ★
Complete Set - $12.00	Order the Complete Set for Only $12

Secret of Fatima Edition
This 2001 edition takes a closer look at the Secret of Fatima, and in particular, the 'Third Secret' which was revealed by the Church on June 26, 2000. Included is the commentary written by Cardinal Ratzinger, which accompanied the secret's release.

Afterlife Edition
This edition examines the actual places of Heaven, Hell and Purgatory through the eyes of the Saints, Mystics, Visionaries, and Blessed Mother herself. Will you be ready come judgment day?

Illumination Edition
This edition focuses on a coming 'day of enlightenment' in which every person on earth will see their souls in the same light that God sees them. Commonly referred to as the 'Warning' or 'Mini-Judgment', many saints and visionaries, particularly the Blessed Mother have spoken about this great event, now said to be imminent.

Eternal Father Edition
This edition makes visible the love and tenderness of God the Father and introduces a special consecration to Him. Many of His messages for the world today tell of the great love He has for all of His 'Prodigal Children.'

Holy Spirit Edition
This edition reveals how the Holy Spirit continues to work through time and history, raising up great saints in the Church. Emphasized in the hidden, yet important role of St. Joseph.

Eucharistic Edition
This edition contains evidence for the Real Presence of Christ in the Eucharist. Many miracles and messages are recorded to reaffirm this truth.

Special Edition III
This edition focuses on the great prophecies the Blessed Mother has given to the world since her apparitions in 1917 at Fatima. Prophetic events related to the 'Triumph of Her Immaculate Heart' are addressed in detail.

Special Edition II
This edition examines the apparitions of the Blessed Mother at Fatima and in relation to today's apparitions occurring worldwide.

Special Edition I
The first in a trilogy of the apparitions and messages of the Blessed Mother, this edition tells why Mary has come to earth and is appearing to all parts of the world today.

Best Sellers by Dr. Thomas W. Petrisko!

Inside Heaven and Hell

What History, Theology and Mystics Tell Us About the Afterlife
Take a spiritual journey with the saints, mystics, visionaries, and the Blessed Mother - inside Heaven and Hell! Discover what really happens at your judgment. With profound new insight into what awaits each one of us, this book is a *must read for all those who are serious about earning their 'salvation.'* $ 14.95

Inside Purgatory

What History, Theology, and the Mystics tell us about Purgatory
The follow up book to the best-seller '*Inside Heaven and Hell*' this books continues on in the same 'reader-friendly' format. Guiding the reader through the teachings of the Church and Scripture, this book is also enhanced by what mystics, visionaries, saints and scholars tell us about this mysterious place. $10.95

The Fatima Prophecies

At the Doorstep of the World
This powerhouse book tells of the many contemporary prophecies and apparitions and how they point to the fulfillment of Fatima's two remaining prophecies, the 'annihilation of nations' and 'era of peace'. Is the world about to enter the era of peace or will there be a terrible chastisement? Contains over 60 pictures. $14.95

The Miracle of the Illumination of All Consciences

Known as the 'Warning' or 'Mini-Judgment' a coming "day of enlightenment" has been foretold. It is purported to be a day in which God will supernaturally illuminate the conscience of every man, woman, and child on earth. Each person, then, would momentarily see the state of their soul through God's eyes and realize the truth of His existence. $12.95

Toll-Free (888) 654-6279 or (412) 787-9735 www.SaintAndrew.com

St. Andrew's Productions Order Form

Order Toll-Free! 1-888-654-6279 or 1-412-787-9735
Visa, MasterCard Accepted!

_____	Call of the Ages (Petrisko)	$12.95
_____	Catholic Answers for Catholic Parents	$ 8.95
_____	Catholic Parents Internet Guide	$ 3.00
_____	Face of the Father, The (Petrisko)	$ 9.95
_____	False Prophets of Today (Petrisko)	$ 7.95
_____	Fatima Prophecies, The (Petrisko)	$14.95
_____	Fatima's Third Secret Explained (Petrisko)	$14.99
_____	Finding Our Father (Centilli)	$ 4.95
_____	Glory to the Father (Petrisko)	$ 8.95
_____	God 2000 (Fr. Richard Foley, SJ)	$11.95
_____	Holy Spirit in the Writings of PJP II	$19.95
_____	In God's Hands (Petrisko)	$12.95
_____	Inside Heaven and Hell (Petrisko)	$14.95
_____	Inside Purgatory (Petrisko)	$10.95
_____	Kingdom of Our Father, The (Petrisko)	$16.95
_____	Last Crusade, The (Petrisko)	$ 9.95
_____	Mary in the Church Today (McCarthy)	$14.95
_____	Miracle of the Illumination, The	$12.95
_____	Prophecy of Daniel, The (Petrisko)	$ 7.95
_____	Prodigal Children, The (Centilli)	$ 4.95
_____	Seeing with the Eyes of the Soul: Vol. 1	$ 3.00
_____	Seeing with the Eyes of the Soul: Vol. 2	$ 3.00
_____	Seeing with the Eyes of the Soul: Vol. 3	$ 3.00
_____	Seeing with the Eyes of the Soul: Vol. 4	$ 3.00
_____	Sorrow, Sacrifice and the Triumph	$13.00
_____	St. Joseph and the Triumph (Petrisko)	$10.95

Cassette
_____ Mary, and the
World Trade Center *(2) 40 min* $10.00

Name:_____

Address:_____

City:_____St_____Zip_____

Phone:_____Fax_____

Visa/MasterCard_____

Total Enclosed:_____

PLEASE ADD SHIPPING/TAX
$0-24.99...$4.00, $25-49.99...$6.00, $50-99.99...$8.00, $100 + Add 8%
PA Residents Add 7% Tax
OR MAIL ORDER TO:
St. Andrew's Productions, 6111 Steubenville Pike, McKees Rocks, PA 15136
www.SaintAndrew.com

www.ingramcontent.com/pod-product-compliance
Lightning Source LLC
LaVergne TN
LVHW041629070426
835507LV00008B/528